Purchasing Performance

T0382807

Dedicated to my Grandchildren
Adam, Sam, Shauna, Greg and Jenny

If your wish is to succeed – 'never, never, never, give up!'
Winston Churchill

Purchasing Performance

Measuring, Marketing and Selling the Purchasing Function

DEREK ROYLANCE

Routledge
Taylor & Francis Group

LONDON AND NEW YORK

First published in paperback 2024

First published 2006 by Gower Publishing

Published 2016 by Routledge
4 Park Square, Milton Park, Abingdon, Oxon OX14 4RN

and by Routledge
605 Third Avenue, New York, NY 10158

Routledge is an imprint of the Taylor & Francis Group, an informa business

Publisher's Note
The publisher has gone to great lengths to ensure the quality of this reprint but points out that some imperfections in the original copies may be apparent.

British Library Cataloguing in Publication Data
Roylance, Derek
Purchasing performance: measuring, marketing and selling
the purchasing function
1. Purchasing 2. Negotiation
I.Title
658.7'2

Library of Congress Cataloging-in-Publication Data
Roylance, Derek, 1938–
Purchasing performance: measuring, marketing, and selling the purchasing function / by Derek Roylance.
p. cm.
Includes index.
ISBN 0-566-08678-6
1. Purchasing departments. 2. Industrial procurement. I. Title.

HF5437.R69 2006
658.7'2--dc22

2005035228

ISBN: 978-0-566-08678-6 (hbk)
ISBN: 978-1-03-283774-1 (pbk)
ISBN: 978-1-315-60306-3 (ebk)

DOI: 10.4324/9781315603063

CONTENTS

FOREWORD

There is an old saying: 'Customers are always right, even when they're wrong.' And what buyer out there has not encountered a Finance Director who has said: 'Show me the money!'

These words go to the heart of Procurement's place in the organization. Can it best grow its influence by applying a central mandate on all purchasing or by marketing itself as though it were an independent internal supplier? Is it the gatekeeper for purchase-to-pay transactions, or is it winning friends and favour through demonstrable expertise in supplier relationships, negotiations and (even) entrepreneurialism? In other words, is Procurement a marketing-led business or a mandate-fuelled function?

For some manufacturing organizations it is already an integral part of the production process at the very least sitting somewhere between production control and the shop floor; and at the very best the vital ingredient in the entire supply chain. So here the debate between mandates and marketing is pretty academic, it is business as usual; and whilst it is embedded in the business it is essentially a function.

But what about the maintenance, repair and operations (MRO) spend? This is not nearly so cut and dried, though the contribution already made to the bottom line should convince any Chief Executive Officer (CEO) of the value of giving Procurement a free rein in all the soft back-office services such as consulting services, marketing, human resources or IT and telecomms. Whilst the debate with MRO is more to do with role and output, it nonetheless demands a business approach, not least with suppliers.

Some buyers are out there demanding the attention of the CEO, *then* delivering. Others are (quietly) winning confidence before delivering. Which approach is better? Is the problem all to do with how to measure the performance and contribution of Procurement? The *mandators* have usually focused narrowly on cost savings – with the optimistic, innovative ones looking for process as well as input savings. The management in a mandated environment then locks in the saving to business units' budgets. At least this way the Financial Director gets his hands on some hard cash.

The *marketeers* have often favoured a wider target concentrating on answering the question: how can Purchasing integrate itself into the fabric of the business unit, in order to deliver not (just) cost savings but the key business objectives such as shareholder value, customer satisfaction, market share and net profit before tax (NPBT) improvement? In this scenario, the business unit keeps any savings and measures instead the cost effectiveness.

Yet Procurement continues to struggle to command the attention of the top table in many organizations. Is there a third way? Is it about seeing Procurement in post-modern terms? I have argued elsewhere about this notion of interpreting and embedding the core elements of postmodernism (essentially the departure from old theories and the embrace of consumerism and mass communication in a post-industrial society) into the fabric of a high-profile procurement strategy, one that engages at the highest levels in the organization. Taking Charles Handy's *Empty Raincoat* paradoxes as a starting point, we can see good procurement practice as virtual; not reliant on process but best exercised through expertise and intelligence.

Is it also about seeing your users as customers, stakeholders even? Users often have little power and low expectations but usually know the ins and outs of the process. By contrast, customers feel empowered and know the destination, even if they don't always comprehend the detailed nuances of the process. Customers are probably harder – but more rewarding – to deal with.

There may still be a case for Procurement to act as the occasional policeman in the process. But more and more, Procurement must act as architect, advisor, trouble-shooter, coach, mentor – essentially as an *Active Consultant*. In this way we still bring core expertise in market development, tendering, contracting, negotiating and vendor management to the table, but we will deliver it through new engagement channels with our customers that not only rely increasingly on better communications abilities, but also inexorably on a wider risk-led skills set.

In my view post-modern purchasing provides a template and context for this expanding skills set; but even more importantly helps us stick to the good practice journey rather than beguiling best practice destinations. I also happen to believe strongly that there is an overwhelming case for treating Procurement as a business operating in an internal market with real products, customers and service levels. It is not a theoretical case; nor is it told from a purely external marketing standpoint. As a buyer all my professional life I have spent the last ten years selling purchasing services to other buyers – real services in a real market for real money. Some of my *corporate* colleagues have been doing something similar for almost as long.

Where does that leave us? Still with lots of questions. Derek's book provides us with some of the answers. It is both a road map and practical guide book for the journey... I hope you enjoy the trip.

David Hewitt
Managing Director
PSL Consulting Solutions Limited
www.pslconsulting.co.uk

ACKNOWLEDGEMENTS

Merely to become involved in the strangely esoteric effort of trying to write a book has forced me to re-evaluate the people and events that have shaped and influenced the opinions, thoughts and convictions that I have tried to commit to paper. Looking back, I feel that even the people that I did not have much opinion of helped me by teaching me how not to do things and the heat of doing battle with them strengthened convictions and sharpened determination.

However, these people are pigmies in comparison to the myriad generous friends that have provided positive influence, help and assistance throughout my buying career. To list just a few I therefore firstly give acknowledgement to my wife and family who gave me the space and encouragement to indulge my literary attempt. To Trevor Kitching who trod this path before me and insisted that I must go for it. To Simon Elvin the most inspirational manager I have ever met and whose technique I have miserably failed to imitate all my life. To Peter Birch who as Chief Executive of Abbey National was the most strategically astute businessman it has been my pleasure to ever observe in action. He led Abbey National from being an old-fashioned building society, through flotation, to at one time being in the top five of UK high street banks. In fact, he was so good that they found him impossible to replace and after his retirement the organisation lost its way and sadly was eventually taken over. To the irascible James Tyrell and gentleman John Fry who gave me the freedom and encouragement to build a group purchasing division. To Ken Halliford and Sandra Kilbane – one taught me a great deal about negotiation, the other how to handle the tears and tantrums of staff. To recruitment team colleagues at CIPS (The Chartered Institute of Purchasing & Supply), Alex, David, Brian and Tim who were a joy to work with and provided a foundation for my fledgling business. To John Ashfield who started out as a purchasing protégé but later followed his natural talents for dealing with people by becoming a hugely successful sales director. To Bill Mallion who generously interrupted a holiday in Italy to give me a master class in non-verbal communication. Lastly, and at the risk of sounding like an Oscar nominee, to colleagues and suppliers at Abbey National (during the glory days), at Image Arts of England (whilst Simon was in charge) and at The Readers Digest Association. (Where are you all now?)

THANKS A MILLION ALL

DR

CHAPTER 1

INTRODUCTION

THE ROLE OF PURCHASING

Some parts of this book are designed to arouse controversy and debate; however, few will disagree that the very essence of the buying process is about consistently locating the best suppliers to provide the best products and services at the best overall value. Just how these admirable goals are achieved is a completely different matter and far more complex than most people envisage. For a start, people are involved, and buying probably forms part of the human genetic matrix because trading is an activity that has been going on throughout the evolution of our species. It is all too often an innate emotional activity that people indulge themselves in and it can lead to business decisions being made based on feelings and subjectivity – something that does not sit well with the training to deal only in facts and objectivity that purchasing professionals receive. Right away we can begin to see a clash of cultures start to develop between internal customers who like to buy intuitively and instinctively and purchasing professionals who are seeking to apply commercial acumen to the process. However, it is the very term 'customer' that dictates it is the purchasing professional who must seek to bridge the gap and persuade internal customers that their expertise is worth employing. Better marketing and sales must be the key – something that the profession has to date not been very good at.

BUYER ATTITUDES

When buyers get together on courses, conferences and the like, even if they are from very diverse backgrounds, it is interesting to observe that the conversation at meal times or in the bar in the evening will nearly always revolve around a couple of recurring themes.

The first frequently discussed theme will inevitably be about ethical issues such as the crooked deals or scams that one or two dubious suppliers are currently hawking around. Stories like someone knows buyer X has accepted from supplier Y a two-weeks all-inclusive holiday in a company apartment in Monaco. Someone else knows about organization Z where brown envelopes are being accepted by buyers in return for the continuation of an overpriced deal for consumables. Gossip about corruption is grist for the mill and will certainly break the ice at any gathering of buyers. However, whilst acknowledging the importance and fascination of the subject, this book will deal with ethical issues in only one chapter: in context, it suggests that maintaining a reputation for the highest business standards is also a vital element in successfully marketing the profession.

The book will, however, address in depth the second recurring theme of buyer to buyer conversations, concerning the claim that the worth of the purchasing function is never adequately rewarded and recognised by top management. The cry always goes up that the profile of buying needs to be raised and better represented at executive level – something that never quite seems to happen in most organizations. Buyers also point out, sometimes with justification, that this lack of top-level representation and recognition is reflected in salary levels being lower than peer group colleagues in other disciplines. Recent salary surveys do not, however, entirely back up this wage gap folklore.

Back in the office at informal gatherings around the photocopier, after the subjects of the latest juicy gossip and office politics have been exhausted, the debate will sometimes turn to work and when this happens will often involve a collective denigration of 'maverick' buyers. In this context the aforesaid office will usually mean a purchasing or buying department with the staff earning their living by being wholly employed in some purchasing related role. They will invariably refer to themselves as purchasing professionals and other people around the organization who undertake some buying as a peripheral part of their main job activity will be labelled amateur, rogue or maverick buyers. The assumption being that professionals should be responsible for all the purchasing because the mavericks do not know what they are doing, the constant cry is 'oh why does the organization not realize this'? We are back to recognition and profile issue again.

THE PROFESSION

If an ambitious young graduate has ambitions to rise to the top, there are far more sales or finance directors on the boards of organizations both large and small than there are purchasing directors – so perhaps their motto should be 'better aim to sell or count young man'!.

The profession has nevertheless achieved tremendous strides over the past few years, especially in the field of raising academic standards and increasing acceptance of the importance of examination results. In the UK for instance the three Chartered Institute of Purchasing & Supply (CIPS) qualifications of Foundation and Professional stage examinations plus the option of a Graduate Diploma have been widely acknowledged as being the yardsticks for measuring and raising professional standards. As evidence of this the majority of job advertisements now specify a requirement for CIPS qualifications. It is not so long ago that Richard Lamming at Bath was ploughing a lone furrow holding the only Chair in Purchasing in a British university; now there are a plethora of Chairs with several universities offering Masters of Business Administration (MBAs) and masters degrees in procurement.

Of course the UK experience is not unique. In the USA the National Association of Purchasing Managers (NAPM) has engineered a similar academic revolution, as have our colleagues in Europe and other parts of the world. The academic progress that the profession has made of late is certainly something to be shouted from the rooftops. The question remains, however: has this academic progress been reflected by the profession operationally? Most of us would say 'not as much as we would like'. There certainly still appears to be some lagging behind in the practical application of the theory in our profession.

Perhaps it can also be said that purchasing management training is currently too narrowly focused on specialist skills exposing a gap in all-round business acumen that may become apparent at the board room strategic level. It can therefore be anticipated that in general a Managing Director would be more likely to accept advice on running the entire business from a Financial rather than a Purchasing Director.

BUYERS AT WORK

There is a wide variety of ways that buying is handled across both the private and public sectors and apart from some basic procedures there is no perfect way of carrying it out. In practice we are employed in a 'horses for courses' profession. Some of us are working in the Stone Age whereas others, such as the automotive, electronic or fast moving consumer goods (FMCG) sectors, are operating in a state-of-the-art supply chain environment.

As examples, consider a lone buyer juggling stock record cards in a small engineering company fire-fighting late deliveries, compared with the sophisticated manufacturing resource planning (MRP) computer systems operated by buyers at Toyota, Ford or Nissan. In the public sector there are also tremendous differences in the way that buyers work. Compare for instance the basic methods employed by some small local authorities with the most advanced areas of NHS procurement. However, at both ends of the scale, whether private or public, the show must go on!

Whilst being cognisant of the wide diversity that exists in the profession, it must be not be used as an excuse to rest on our laurels and give up on pushing the profession forward across the board. There are many acknowledged but neglected best-in-class methods that can be made to work in most purchasing environments, given application and effort. Few for instance would disagree with the statement that 'purchasing is more effective working proactively rather than reactively'. In other words, the earlier buyers get involved, the better the outcome. We all know this but how many of us are still spending far too much time chasing our tails and fire-fighting?

Buyers as a whole will quite rightly preach the message of objectivity and fact-based decision making. However, as human beings, try as we might, we cannot ignore the fact that emotions and feelings will inevitably also be part of the equation, often at a subconscious level. Sales people are trained to understand and exploit these hidden and silent parts of the human psyche. By the same token buyers who wish to improve their people skills would also do well to equip themselves with the means of interpreting the subtle silent messages that we give out and receive all the time using our body language.

SKILLS

If we define the profession as consisting of people who earn their living by being involved in buying, there are tremendous differences in the skills and expertise levels available.

On the one hand there is a requirement for a great deal more training of existing staff which is properly targeted to meet job needs as organizations adopt a more enlightened view of procurement. On the other hand it is pointless parachuting in bright, highly qualified young graduates if top management do not have the vision to organize a progressive career structure to employ them effectively.

MEASURING

Traditionally the profession as a whole has not been very good at measuring its own performance. When consultancy work is being undertaken, it is a constant surprise that when buyers are asked how much their spend is per annum they often struggle to come up with an answer. Surprising because most buyers will readily acknowledge that without having basic figures available such as:

- *how much?* (Total spend)
- *who is spending it?* (The decision makers)
- *on what?* (Products or services purchased – spend on each commodity grouping)
- *with whom?* (Spend with each supplier)

it is impossible to even begin to assess the contribution that the function is making to the organization. In the commercial world the major aim of purchasing should be to contribute to increasing both profit and competitive advantage. Translated into public sector parlance these major aims are to stretch budgets further, or even underspend them, coupled with striving to achieve continuous improvement in the quality of the goods and services obtained.

Even if buyers do take on board the importance of performance measurement, and computerization is making the financial analysis much easier, unless the information is presented to internal customers in an attractive and interesting manner, significant progress will not be achieved.

MARKETING AND SELLING

Buyers are wasting their time constantly complaining about their status within the organization being low and that their skills are not being recognized unless they are prepared to question why and decide what they can do about it. The first question must be: how good is purchasing at marketing itself? The answer must be: not very good, because very often it is far too busy reacting to external events that come along as a series of continual surprises. Some people even enjoy fire-fighting and treasuring piles of paper work!

It is far more comfortable to focus one's gaze externally when suppliers, desperate to gain attention and influence, strive to make life easy and pleasant at all times for the buyer. By contrast, internal customer colleagues can be difficult and extremely demanding in their expectations of the buyer. No wonder therefore that there is a preference to spend more time than may be strictly necessary on looking outside the organization, but this is at the risk of neglecting and alienating internal colleagues who collectively pay the wages and affect career prospects.

It becomes paramount to make progress that Purchasing as a function must re-orientate itself to pay more attention to the internal dynamics of the organization. This initially means finding out precisely what internal customers are requiring – their true wants and needs – *marketing*. This information is then used to promote and present an offer in such a way that it is irresistible to the customer – *sales*.

Fortunately it is not necessary to re-invent the wheel, especially when buyers experience sales and marketing techniques from the other side of the fence nearly every day of their working lives. Practical application is, however, not as simple as it may first appear.

DEALING WITH PEOPLE

With sales people constantly beating a path to the door with the objective of making friends by being extremely complimentary about the buyers' every whim, it is hardly surprising that buyers are not used to making much effort to establish relationships. Taking on sales and marketing aspirations is, however, a different matter entirely because, with the shoe on the other foot, people skills become vital for achieving success. Buyers tend to underestimate and even decry the soft selling skills that are practised on them every day but it is essential for them to master them in order to positively influence the outcome of any relationship-building objective. This is the reason for the chapter on body language, because a basic understanding will provide an insight to people's subconscious feelings that are such an important part of all human face-to-face communication.

THE FUTURE

It is not too difficult to predict that the purchasing profession will in future be subjected to tremendous changes, but precisely what they will be no one can tell. It does appear, however, that in an ever-faster moving world the conventional departmental box-like structure that most organizations currently operate is a barrier to efficiency. The breakdown of these barriers could therefore lead to a move to more project-based methods of working, with traditional departmental style job demarcation becoming extremely blurred at the edges. It is therefore likely that in future, generalist business management skills will be in much more demand than specialist skills.

With regard to a question of semantics, some purists may take exception to the way that the words buying, purchasing and procurement are used in more or less the same context throughout this book. Whilst acknowledging that strictly speaking this is not always correct, these three words are nevertheless usually interchangeable in a workplace setting. Above all, the aim of the author is to offer practical down-to-earth advice.

CHAPTER 2

THE MANAGEMENT ROLE

A PERSONAL VIEW OF MANAGING PEOPLE

Most people in the workplace do not like change and will inevitably be initially resistant. As this book advocates major changes in the way that purchasing teams operate, it is as well to examine the role that management, as the major catalyst, must fulfil.

What is the definition of a manager? The IBM definition: is anybody who has one or more persons reporting to them is a manager. Everyone who has made that first step, perhaps to become a supervisor, will remember the experience very well. Most of us initially thought that we could remain mates with our colleagues on the shop floor but soon discovered that it did not work, as they either resented our promotion or took liberties with the friendship. It was difficult to withdraw slightly without them saying that we were taking on airs and graces, but we soon learnt that it was essential to maintain a slight distance if we were ever to make an impact on managing and leading people.

Managers are encouraged (quite rightly) to constantly 'stroke' and praise staff as part of a successful team-building process, but quickly learn to become resigned to not receiving much in return. Everyone always thinks that they can do a better job than their line manager. Any praise that managers do receive tends to be of an 'obituary' nature. By 'obituary' I mean that it is extraordinary how managers suddenly become marvellous people and great leaders when they leave or die! Perhaps this is a somewhat cynical illustration of the need for budding managers to be self-confident, pragmatic and even thick-skinned.

To some extent I am of the school that believes that great managers are like great teachers – they are born not made. But there again, who am I to judge when I never made it to be anywhere near being Managing Director of a large organization? Managing 100 staff was the height of my achievement and was quite enough to stretch me to the limit and beyond!

The cut and thrust of operational buying is exciting and stimulating so, when taking the first tentative steps into management, people often find it difficult to delegate. After all we all usually feel that nobody else can do the job as well as we can. Of course the problem is reduced if we have good people to delegate to and in this respect the importance of effective relevant training cannot be overemphasized.

As managers take on more responsibility, the sheer amount of work on hand means that just to survive on the hours available in the day, delegation becomes a necessity. The danger is then that managers can abdicate from important operational matters by becoming remote from their people because they become trapped in apparently more weighty matters such as budgets, long-term planning and worst of all organizational politics. There is a fine line between delegation and abdication that the best managers pay heed to by constant self-analysis of how their management style is playing out with their people. Communication is key, firstly by walking the floor every day and talking, and more importantly listening, to staff about their work and their life outside work. Delegation is about trust and giving someone else the freedom to do the job, but it is also about communication; therefore clear guidelines need to be laid down on just what they must still report and provide feedback on. Boundaries also need to be established that will be different for different people, if nothing else because in my experience common sense is anything but a universally common trait. I well recall a young, rather arrogant and self-important buyer coming to me with a supplier problem that had all the hallmarks of escalating into a major show-stopping incident that could show Purchasing in a very bad light. I said to him not to worry as I had known the Managing Director of the company for many years and if that failed my boss had a similarly good relationship with the Chairman. My young man then astonished me by saying that he had already admonished both the Managing Director and the Chairman and was quite surprised that he had received a flea in his ear. My angry retort to him was to ask what he wanted me to do as he had left me with nowhere to go – should I perhaps employ a magic wand? It took a great deal of time, diplomacy and calling in favours on my part from the Managing Director to retrieve the situation. Before this incident I had assumed that the departmental culture was one where buyers and managers used their collective power to achieve the best results. Wrong. My young buyer obviously required a different set of guidelines from the rest. Incidentally, I am prepared to bet that my young buyer, though no longer young, still has failed to learn any common sense.

Everyone has their own innate management style depending on personality and the ways they have devised to interact with people that have been absorbed as part of the growing up process. Some are quiet, some are loud, extrovert or introvert. It is nigh on impossible to change our innate basic style, but we can build on our strengths and learn coping systems to mask our weaknesses. For instance, when I first managed a medium sized department I just did not know how to handle some women who, when I was discussing difficult work situations with them, had a tendency to burst into tears. Inevitably I would not know how to react, turn into a gibbering wreck and totally fail to get my point across. Maybe it was because I was brought up in a family consisting of one brother and attended an all boys school? Eventually I discussed my failing with a female manager colleague who laughed and said 'that's an easy one to deal with: just take no notice and carry on as normal'. She then added 'should they threaten to flood my desk I may make a slight concession by handing out a tissue'! The great thing about that advice is that it worked – every time.

What is certain is that as managers, whatever our style and way of operating, we all stand or fall depending on the performance of our staff. They are our greatest assets, and at times our greatest trial, but working constantly to improve the ways that we communicate with them is the key to success. To return to the first theme of this chapter – when persuading people to accept and embrace change – it is impossible to give them too much information.

THE DIFFERENCE BETWEEN BUYERS AND SHOPPERS

In life generally it appears that everyone considers himself or herself to be an expert driver, lover and buyer – three areas in which it is very difficult for anyone to accept personal criticism. Whilst readily acknowledging that the first two aspects of this life expertise may be more interesting, they are beyond the remit of this book. Therefore to return to buying, purchasing managers often find it difficult to promote the benefits of professionalism because the people they are talking to think that they already know all about the subject anyway.

People will readily accept that the main reason they are employed is because they have skills that are needed by the organization. Someone perhaps working in accounts will willingly acknowledge that they do not know about marketing and that the organization needs to employ people with different skills than their own to work in the marketing arena. Not so with purchasing – everyone, but everyone, considers themselves to be expert at buying. The reason I guess is that we all spend money every day, but there is a big difference between merely spending one's own money shopping in the high street and efficiently buying on behalf of a business. Better they consider themselves to be expert *Shoppers* and leave the buying to specialist *Buyers.*

Under these circumstances it is important to examine and place these irrational notions about purchasing into some sort of context. How then to classify the difference between professional buyers and others in different vocations for whom buying is only a peripheral activity? Traditionally real buyers will refer derisively to these people as being amateurs. However, a clearer distinction is to classify people who spend an organization's money into *Shoppers* or *Buyers.*

Shoppers are people who make their buying decisions based on their emotions and feelings. For example, they will choose a product because they find the sales person's style appealing. Sellers love people who let their feelings dominate their decisions because they are much easier to manipulate. Shoppers tend to make irrational *subjective* decisions.

Buyers are people who make their buying decisions based on facts, not feelings or emotions. They are not impulsive and will carefully weigh all the alternatives before deciding. Buyers will check out what a sales person tells them and make their decisions based on the facts and qualities that can be measured and compared. Buyers make rational, measurable *objective* decisions.

Be aware, however, that even the most expert Buyer will also become a Shopper sometimes. For example, when buying clothes for ourselves we will usually become a Shopper making decisions based on personal feelings like style, fashion, and whether it makes us look good. The chain store Buyer that procured the merchandise will, however, have made purchasing decisions based on facts such as availability, cost, profit margins, cloth quality, wear properties, colour fastness, and so on.

The trick is never to indulge in Shopping when spending the organization's money!

MANAGING PURCHASING POSITIONING AND DEVELOPMENT

We acknowledge that people are our best asset but they need leadership to achieve common goals and vision to identify and promote the benefits that optimization of the procurement function can bring to the organization.

An obvious way of planning for the future is firstly to take a step back and objectively examine the current positioning of Purchasing both within the organization but also within the spectrum of potential that the function can progress to. The development of procurement can be viewed in an historical or evolutionary context. The spread is from a low-level, subservient position right up to a high-level, world-class supply chain management position, plus all shades of grey in between. Viewed from an historical position, for instance, when Alec Isigonis designed the first Mini in 1955 engineers held the power in the old Austin Morris motor group. Most will say, 'great car of its time', but with engineers controlling the costing no wonder it hardly ever made any substantial profits for the organization. Contrast that with the currently very successful and profitable BMW successor to the original Mini where a world-class procurement function is an essential part of producing a profitable product of international appeal.

Similarly viewed from an evolutionary viewpoint, one can envisage a small company just starting out which begins a buying function just to take pressure off the production manager; but imagine they hit the jackpot and design an innovative product that in ten years' time will be sold worldwide. To keep up with this kind of success it is inevitable that over the ten years the buying function will by necessity evolve into a world-class supply chain management operation.

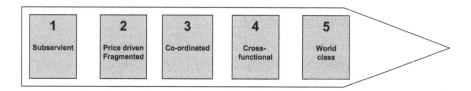

Figure 2.1   The evolution of purchasing

The spread of evolutionary purchasing development can be viewed in five stages, though it should be emphasized that there are no distinct boundaries between the stages. The edges are blurred and can be further complicated because it is perfectly possible to, say, be world class in some respects but only co-ordinated in others. The stages are:

1. Subservient
2. Price driven and fragmented
3. Co-ordinated
4. Cross-functional
5. World-class supply management

1. Subservient

This is the initial stage where a person/people are employed to merely keep buying operations running, be it in the manufacturing or service sectors, private or public. Typically they will operate at business unit or site level.

Role
To provide buying back-up to an operational manager who retains the right to make the key purchasing decisions. Will report to that operational manager and is more or less at their beck and call.

Organizational position
Has little buying responsibility except as a mere extension of the operational manager's power.

Key skills
Clerical and logistical.

Typical activity
Find suppliers usually locally, raise orders, progress chase, maintain stock levels, general administration.

2. Price driven and fragmented

As the organization realizes the importance of controlling its cost structure, purchasing is charged with reducing spend. It begins to emerge as a separate area that is judged on its ability to find low-cost suppliers and using competitive tendering and tough negotiation to reduce prices. Business units will tend to still operate independently thereby fragmenting potential buying power.

Role
To provide buying expertise at a business unit level. Will tend to still report to an operational manager and remain a reactive downstream operation.

Organizational position
Will be recognized as possessing buying expertise by experience and possibly by qualification.

Key skills
Negotiation, knowledge of marketplace, preparation of invitations to tender, cost analysis, ability to use computer systems, expediting, fire-fighting.

Typical activity
Drive down costs by finding cheaper sources, use cost analysis in negotiation, manage bidding and control inventory, promote good relations with suppliers on a day-to-day basis.

3. Co-ordinated purchasing

As realization grows of the role that efficient procurement can play in increasing both bottom-line contribution and competitive advantage, taking advantage of economies of scale leverage becomes more attractive. Lower costs can be achieved by pooling business unit spend by centralizing the purchasing operation. There will be a need for national contracts and multi-site agreements. It is at this stage, however, where territorial disputes begin to rear their ugly heads, with users accusing a central department of being overbureaucratic while purchasing people seeing this as merely an excuse for users to indulge in maverick buying (doing their own thing).

Role
To provide economies of scale advantages by pulling procurement spend together from across the organization. Centralized purchasing departments have a tendency to hang onto mountains of administration but nevertheless make inroads into taking a more proactive approach and do become involved in influencing organizational strategy.

Organizational position
Will either be a centralized purchasing unit or a tightly controlled cross-unit federation of several business units. Will tend to report to board level, typically the financial director. Buyers will be professionally qualified.

Key skills
Ability to negotiate national contracts, databases are employed to analyse the marketplace, introduction of commodity management.

Typical activity
Work with internal customers to manage procurement decisions. Police corporate procurement policies. Use economies of scale leverage to advantage. Build relationships with key suppliers. Maintain a watch on supplier key cost drivers such as raw material price movements. Evaluation of second and third tier supplier bases.

4. Cross-functional purchasing

Centralized purchasing in a profit centre managed environment can lead to disputes with the business unit managers complaining that they lose control of their expenditure and therefore cannot be held accountable when profits do not meet targets. Organizations also realize that good realistic design, accurate specifications and co-operative supplier development have far more impact on cost structures than traditional buyer/seller negotiation. This leads to a cross-functional team-working environment with Purchasing playing a vital strategic role, particularly with regard to the commercial aspects. The 'them and us' confrontations of centralization are thus removed from the equation.

Role
To provide centre-led procurement strategies whilst relinquishing day-to-day operations to be executed in business units. The service may or may not be operated at a Group head office level. The procurement manager position will be at a senior, possibly board level.

Organizational position
Recognized as being a key player in formulating overall business strategy.

Key skills
Business skills required in addition to procurement expertise, supplier development, effective communication and persuasive abilities.

Typical activity
Performance measurement of processes and suppliers, supplier evaluation and accreditation, make versus buy decisions, challenging specifications,

continuous improvement programmes, lifetime cost analysis. Lead negotiation of major contracts.

5. World-class supply management

This development has been led by cutting-edge automotive, electronic and fast moving goods organizations realizing that it pays to operate globally and they must therefore employ or develop world class suppliers. Purchasing is characterized typically in terms of cross-functional supplier development teams, co-sponsored design, long-term supplier relationships including risk sharing and selective equity investment and collaboration in introducing new technology. To succeed in this environment a buyer must become and all-round business animal.

Role
To provide organization of procurement and the supply chain that complements the high standards of an acknowledged world class organization. Operates at strategic levels covering procurement aspects on everything from design to after sales service.

Organizational position
Board-level recognition as being crucial to maintain a best-in-class position such as time to market considerations. Confident in ability to handle business decisions globally across all cultures. Works in cross-functional teams with suppliers as well as in own organization.

Key skills
International business experience, ability to play a leading role in cross-functional teams, design out cost expertise, entrepreneurial global viewpoint.

Typical activity
Establishing new sources of supply in emerging markets, continuous improvement measures of supplier performance, sophisticated reverse marketing, collaboration with suppliers to introduce advanced technology, work on advantageous supplier partnerships or co-located production.

The above is an attempt to produce a generic interpretation of purchasing evolution and development. However, the criteria may in practice vary by market sector, but in general similar principles will apply and form a basis for assessing the current position of Purchasing and signpost realistic aspirations for development. At a practical level each of the five stages may be appropriate for some organizations, depending on their current general organizational development, and it is not therefore automatically correct to assume that it is vital to progress to the next stage. For instance, it is pointless to attempt to build a world class purchasing unit for an organization that is struggling to exist in a local environment. Even in cases like this it may nevertheless be worthwhile examining the model and using it to progress some areas on a pick-and-mix basis. Furthermore it can be strongly argued that for the majority of medium and large size organizations it is beneficial and eminently possible to move procurement activity to the cross-functional stage, especially if the measuring and marketing programmes advocated later in this book are employed.

TAKING A STRATEGIC VIEW OF PROCUREMENT

The bulk of this book is about promoting purchasing excellence via measured proof of effectiveness and subsequent marketing and selling to internal customers. However, it needs to be established firstly that there is already in place something that is worth selling – something that internal customers can appreciate is of positive benefit. Earlier in this chapter a tool is supplied to examine positioning within the organization. Fairly obviously, it is relatively easy for any maverick manager to set up and operate a subservient form of buying, but most would not begin to even have a clue what the term world class supply management encompasses. It behoves us therefore to strive to provide some expertise that the Shoppers in the organization cannot easily lay their hands on. In modern parlance we need to be able to offer a strategic package. A definition of strategic purchasing is that procurement needs to be moved away from its traditional role of being a downstream, reactive, service function to being one of an upstream, forward thinking, top-level partner within the organization.

At the moment it is almost impossible to open a trade magazine like *Supply Management* without being bombarded with articles full of the buzz words 'strategic purchasing management'. All this theory is in strange contrast to what I actually find on the ground in a consultancy role. I am amazed to learn that most of the organizations I deal with still do not have a clue on their total annual spend on goods and services, let alone split down by commodity grouping. Many of them then compound my incredibility by advertising for Strategic Purchasing Managers to achieve their world-class aspirations. For goodness sake, if an organization does not know how much it is spending, who is spending it, on what and with whom, they should forget even mentioning the word 'strategic' in a procurement context. OK, it may be difficult information to gather – purchasing systems are often an inefficient tag on to finance systems and robber maverick barons may jealously guard departmental buying information about their domains. If all else fails it may even be necessary to employ an independent consultant to weed out the facts.

Once the figures are available, strategic decisions can begin to be made of how the procurement of various commodities needs to be organized. The most effective tool to use is a good old Boston matrix to prioritize the importance of commodities (bought-in goods and services) to the organization in order to make decisions on supply management and allocation of resources.

Strategic Analysis

	BOTTLENECK ITEMS (Box C)	STRATEGIC ITEMS (Box A)
HIGH	**Focus** – Fast, reliable local supply **Sources** – High reputation, trustworthy **Horizon** – Long term **Items** – Both standard and specialized **Supply** – Selective or scarce **Decision** – Mainly decentralized	**Focus** – Value, reliability, long term availability **Sources** – Established partners **Horizon** – Up to 10 years **Items** – Vital and high value **Supply** – Best suppliers may be scarce **Decision** - Centralized
I M P O R T A N C E	NON-CRITICAL ITEMS (Box D) **Focus** – Functional availability **Sources** – Typically established local **Horizon** – 12 months or less **Items** – Off the shelf **Supply** – Abundant **Decision** – Central contracts or de-centralized	LEVERAGE ITEMS (Box B) **Focus** – Cost/price, availability, choice **Sources** – Multiple suppliers **Horizon** – Variable **Items** – Mainly standard **Supply** – Abundant **Decision** – Centrally co-ordinated
LOW	SPEND	HIGH

Figure 2.2   Strategic analysis Boston matrix

In this model commodities are split into four groupings by analysing importance to the organization on one axis and spend on the other. Common sense therefore tells us that a purchasing manager would be extremely foolish to ignore items that are very important to the organization which also carry a high spend. More sophisticated prioritization can be carried out depending on where exactly an item is positioned within the box. For example, for strategic items that fall in box A, an item that is positioned in the top right hand corner should receive more management attention than one that falls in the bottom left hand corner.

Once commodities have been box positioned, the strategic procurement implications can then be considered with regard to matters such as supplier management, resource allocation, contract length and so on.

Strategically important items (Box A)

These commodities are ones that are high spend and vital to the success of the organization. Delivery failure is a showstopper because these are the commodities that deliver bottom-line and competitive advantage contribution.

- *Supply focus* – Best-in-class suppliers, reliability and high quality essential.
- *Supply sources* – Ensure long-term availability.
- *Time horizons* – Long-term planning.
- *Operational approach* – Build co-operation, trust and loyalty, seen as valued partners. You are good people to do business with. Careful contingency planning.
- *Supply availability* – Best suppliers may be scarce.
- *Decision making* – Taken at senior level.
- *Resource allocation* – Employ the most highly experienced staff with excellent communication skills. Management time priority.

Leverage items (Box B)

These commodities are high spend, usually standard items that are not critical in terms of contributing to the success of the organization. Opportunities here to supply cost-cutting contribution to the bottom line.

- *Supply focus* – Standard products. Lowering prices and ensuring availability.
- *Supply sources* – Plenty to choose from – play the market.
- *Time horizons* – Short to medium.
- *Operational approach* – Firm but fair. More arms length and demanding. Ruthless when necessary. Some items will be ideal for reverse auctions.
- *Supply availability* – Short lead time abundance.
- *Decision making* – Co-ordinated economies of scale planning.
- *Resource allocation* – Use tough negotiators – buyers that can adopt a Rottweiler approach!

Critical bottleneck items (Box C)

Low spend but operationally important. For instance, a plumber that will always be available at very short notice around the clock or vital machine part stocking.

- *Supply focus* – Utterly reliable usual local supply.
- *Supply sources* – Pick trustworthy highly reputable suppliers.
- *Time horizons* – Long term.
- *Operational approach* – Pay over the odds if necessary, foster loyalty – send them a Christmas card! Agree contingency buffer stock holdings.
- *Supply availability* – The best may be hard to find.
- *Decision making* – Use people who are close to the action but back them up with commercial expertise.
- *Resource allocation* – Use people close to the front line with local knowledge but train them on procurement best practice.

Non-critical items (Box D)

These are low spend, low importance commodities such as general stationery that should receive low priority with regard to allocation of resources. These commodities make little or no contribution to either bottom-line or competitive advantage.

- *Supply focus* – Standard products, use satisfactory non-branded alternatives.
- *Supply sources* – Plenty to choose from, typically local.
- *Time horizons* – Review contracts every 12 to 24 months.
- *Operational approach* – Arrange call off single source contracts. Cut or eliminate stock holdings. Try reverse auctions for baskets of items.
- *Supply availability* – Usually off the shelf.
- *Decision making* – Co-ordinated economies of scale planning.
- *Resource allocation* – Ideal for junior buyers to cut their teeth on.

When evaluating buyer CVs it is surprising to see the number that list under their achievement success in buying stationery – often quoting 15 or 20 per cent savings obtained. It makes me question 20 per cent of what and should they have not spent the time far more gainfully employed? Given poor management, buying departments will often spend far too much time looking after Box C or D items, probably because they are the easiest to deal with. However, if the Boston matrix tool is used properly it will concentrate minds and resources on the areas of greatest return. A rough breakdown is that Box A should account for 50 per cent of resources, Box B 30 per cent with only 20 per cent expended jointly on Boxes C and D.

Chapter summary

- It is difficult to change one's basic management style but weaknesses can be modified.

- It can be useful to define professionalism in a Buyer versus Shopper context.

- Analyse potential progress in terms of positioning Purchasing within the organization.

- Use a Boston matrix to formulate commodity supply management strategies.

- Strategic purchasing is about moving the function from being a downstream and reactive operation to being an upstream and proactive key player vital to ensuring organizational success.

CHAPTER 3

THE PROFIT AND LOSS MEASUREMENT SYSTEM

WHY ARE SALES PEOPLE BETTER REWARDED?

Some people say that sales people are paid more than buyers as it is easy to know their worth to the organization because it is relatively simple to assess if they are doing a good job or not. The old maxim: 'Sack 'em if they are not meeting sales targets by bringing in profitable orders' does to some extent still apply. Buyers cannot be measured in the same way. Simplistic perhaps, but it does make the point that it is much harder for top management to judge that their purchasing people are doing a good job. Actually, the case of buyers having a chip on their shoulder regarding pay is becoming less relevant because surveys prove that they have been catching up quite a lot over recent years.

As a profession we have not been very good at measuring our performance, therefore we can hardly gripe when sales people come to call in their latest up market BMWs whilst we are driving around in ancient Nissans. Indeed many complacent buyers are privately happy with the status quo, relieved that they do not have to meet the same type of rigorous performance targets that their sales colleagues are required to hit – even if it does mean a lower salary. Small wonder therefore if some purchasing departments that mire themselves in this sort of mediocrity are considered to be more of a hindrance than a help by other work colleagues.

A company will not survive very long, let alone expand, if it does not sell itself effectively by bringing in a steady stream of customers to buy the products or services that it offers. A successful sales operation can therefore carry a poorly performing purchasing area for some time before the winds of competition begin to make their mark. Eventually, however, sales momentum will not be maintained if costs are not controlled and quality improved.

In this context it is somewhat ironical that top management often will not have much handle on the efficiency of their buying operation. Under these circumstances the function tends to fall into a limbo of being somehow a necessity that provides very little by way of strategic value. In addition if their Purchasing department prefers to perform in a reactive rather than a proactive manner, can top management really be blamed?

To effect fundamental changes in attitudes it is beneficial to think of purchasing operating on a commercial basis as a business within a business. Two principal drivers in any business are sales and finance – two areas that Purchasing tend to steer clear of except in the narrow field of supply side costs. The most appealing product that Purchasing has to sell the organization is additional bottom-line profit, but to clinch the sale better, more universally accepted measures of effectiveness are required. Operating along business within a business principles, a set of accounts will be required, especially a profit and loss (P&L) account – fortunately, something that most top management will understand and appreciate.

HOW A P&L PURCHASING MEASUREMENT SYSTEM WORKS

Most Purchasing Departments will maintain and report some sort of financial record on cost savings that are achieved and be rightly proud of the success. It is therefore disappointing when the eyes of their colleagues, especially at senior level, often glaze over with boredom and incredulity when Purchasing Department savings are discussed. Perhaps it has something to do with the fact that the costs associated with the running of a purchasing department are rarely mentioned in the same breath, therefore they instinctively do not trust the figures. Somehow, it is as if the two parties are not talking the same language; therefore we need to think very carefully about addressing the problem by presenting our findings in a format that is more familiar to the rest of the organization.

Consider: why do organizations employ buyers – what do we have that they want? In their eyes we can take care of areas such as handling the administration, the contractual processes, expediting and so on, jobs that no one else has the inclination to do. However, what the organization really wants to buy from Purchasing is profit contribution. Let us therefore show them what a bargain they are buying by presenting purchasing contribution to organizational success in a financial accounting manner – the P&L system.

It is not difficult to produce a profit and loss account for a Purchasing Department and if it is split down to reporting by individual procurement teams it can also be an excellent staff motivator.

TURNOVER – (total annual purchasing spend)   £s_____

PROFIT – (EXPERTISE CONTRIBUTION)

Price reductions	£s	
Cost savings	£s	
Revised spec. initiatives	£s	
Improved terms	£s	
Buyer innovation and new ideas	£s	
Logistics and inventory savings	£s	
Packaging savings	£s	
Increased admin. efficiency	£s	
Supplier development results	£s	
Volume related discount negotiation	£s	
Savings against trade guide residuals	£s	
Sub total		£s

GROSS PROFIT – total expertise cost savings   **£s_____**

DIRECT COSTS – LABOUR

Wages	£s	
Overtime, travel and subsistence	£s	
Pensions, NI and other e.g., health insurance	£s	
Training	£s	
Sub total		£s_____

INDIRECT COSTS

Rent and rates	£s	
Insurance	£s	
Light, heat and power	£s	
Telephones and IT	£s	
Repairs and maintenance	£s	
Miscellaneous	£s	
Depreciation on capital equipment	£s	
Sub total		£s_____

NETT PROFIT (SAVING) Contribution to bottom line   **£s_____**

P&L account notes

Gross profit (saving) on turnover	__%
Net profit (saving) on turnover	__%
Average net profit per Purchasing employee	**£s_____**
Average salary per Purchasing employee	**£s_____**

Figure 3.1   Matrix for setting up a P&L account for Purchasing

A Procurement profit and loss account classifies total annual purchase spend as the departmental *turnover*. Against this figure the total of genuine cost savings made by Purchasing is expressed as the *gross profit* contribution, but to arrive at a more realistic performance indicator the *nett profit* figure is calculated by deducting the costs of running the department by way of *direct* and *indirect costs*. By using this system procurement performance results can now be expressed in a format that work colleagues from top management to the bean counters are familiar with and can therefore begin to appreciate.

Notes on profit (expertise contribution) categories

It is important to emphasize that all the figures presented must be genuine and can be factually proven, because there will always be plenty of 'smart alecs' and cynics queuing up to shoot holes in them. Be very careful therefore to produce very detailed rules and guidelines on what are and what are not genuine savings. A departmental system must also be set up to subsequently independently verify all expertise contribution claims by buyers and to ensure that sufficient documentation has been produced to back it up. The documentation should be of a sufficient calibre to satisfy the scrutiny of external independent auditors.

- *Price reductions*   This is genuine when a buyer sources or negotiates a cheaper price for a previously purchased commodity procured in similar volumes. It is not genuine if a buyer receives a number of quotes, selects the cheapest and claims it as a saving against the others.
- *Cost savings*   This can cover a multitude of the application of buyer skills as a generic category or it can be split down more specifically as partially undertaken in the P&L matrix example (Figure 3.1). Be careful, however, not to double count, for example if a buyer initiative results in the Finance department cutting its consumption of copier paper by 25 per cent it could be included here. However, if it also results in a 25 per cent reduction of copier paper usage in the Purchasing department, this should not be included in this category as it would be picked up in a reduction of indirect costs.
- *Revised specification initiatives*   Cost savings that are achieved when the buyer suggests and sells specification changes, or different methods of working, which are accepted by the internal customer.
- *Improved terms*   This can cover items such as abolishment of upfront fees, extension of payment due time and so on. If cash flow is healthy it can also cover prompt payment discounts negotiated by buyers.

However, to calculate the true worth of these changes to the organization it will probably require the assistance of the Finance Department. Bank base rates, opportunity costs and so on spring to mind.

- *Buyer innovation and new ideas*   This is a wonderful category to encourage the buyer to think outside the box. Creative innovative buyers can save a fortune by constantly reviewing developments in the marketplace and by suggesting ways on how these developments can be beneficially adopted by the organization.
- *Logistical and Inventory Savings*   Savings achieved by buyers considering and examining the entire supply chain to come up with ideas to streamline the processes. Better inventory management to cut cost should also be an area of permanent continuous improvement for every buyer.
- *Packaging savings*   This is an area where a switched on buyer with good technical knowledge can often make a killing and maybe also help the environment. Supermarket buyers please note!
- *Supplier development results*   For organizations with vibrant supplier development programmes this is an ideal category to record the financial contribution made by purchasing people in increasing supply side efficiency.
- *Volume-related discounts*   Buyers should be conditioned to negotiate extra discounts as volumes grow. Also, if they investigate buying patterns across the organization they will often discover economies of scale opportunities that are ripe for exploitation.
- *Trade Guide residual increase*   Some buyers are responsible for the disposal of second-hand equipment and some markets, for example the used car market, have published Guides recognized by the trade as providing reliable price information. When buyers beat the guide price they make a profit contribution. Conversely they can also make a loss if the Guide price is not obtained – a great tool for sorting the men out from the boys! It may also be valid to compare costs against raw materials, fuel and factory gate prices compared with official published statistics.

INTRODUCING AND USING THE SYSTEM

Initially it is not always easy to convince people either inside the Purchasing Department or outside of the merits of this fairly radical approach. The best champion, source of information and credibility reinforcer is the Finance

Director and frankly where else can reliable figures for such items as for the apportionment per square metre of rent and rates be obtained? The enthusiastic backing of the Finance Director for the approach also opens the doors at Board level. Buy-in by purchasing colleagues is best obtained by laying down a challenge and an implied threat. So: 'You are always saying how good you are, now prove it' and the tough approach: 'The organization wants to know whether it is worth continuing to pay out for your bottoms to be sitting on its chairs.'

It was mentioned earlier that the P&L system is a great staff motivator especially when each commodity team produces individual Profit & Loss forecasts and reports actual results on a regular basis. Do not forget to apportion purchasing management costs to each team. Team performance can then be easily accumulated into a departmental Profit & Loss Report for upward circulation. The P&L system can also be made to dovetail nicely into all the other buyer performance measures in place, such as regular appraisals and management by objectives (see Chapter 4).

Embracing the system leads to startling cultural changes to purchasing commodity teams, perhaps best summed up by the emergence of a 'switch the lights off' mentality. Staff quickly realize that team net profit contribution can be improved if the indirect costs under their control are reduced. Under these circumstances it is easy to stimulate a philosophy of each team working as a business within a business. In the case of a very small department there is no reason why the system should not be based on individual buyers rather than teams.

Once the system has been established it can be expanded to provide more information that can be published by way of an annual Report and Accounts document for Purchasing. It pays to make it look professional using the same house style as the annual Company Report. Perhaps it may be overambitious and demand too much creative accounting to produce a complete balance sheet but there is plenty of room to introduce many meaningful and relevant statistics such as:

- proportion to total organizational turnover (the total annual expenditure on products and services) managed by Purchasing, expressed in financial and percentage figures against the total expenditure incurred by the whole organization on goods and services;
- breakdowns of turnover and net profit by internal customer;

- breakdowns of purchases not managed by Purchasing. Therefore highlighting by implication the lack of financial control elsewhere;
- breakdowns of turnover and net profit by purchasing team;
- average turnover and net profit per staff member;
- numbers and average value of purchase orders and contracts placed;
- growth, including breakdown of new business gained;
- employee report by staff team numbers, direct and indirect costs;
- numbers of professionally trained staff plus training plans;
- top twenty suppliers by orders and value;
- strategic report on the marketplace and key suppliers;
- future plans.

The system once proven will also provide the leverage for the work of Purchasing to become more fully integrated into the organization's strategic planning processes. It is a huge advantage to the organization when preparing annual budgets and longer-term plans that Purchasing can predict, on the basis of expenditure budgets, the additional profit contribution that the function can bring. The downside is that this financial transparency will make them much more accountable – but this should be viewed as just another driver to improve efficiency. No gain without pain!

This system to gain recognition of the financial contribution of Purchasing is not, however, for the faint-hearted. Recently my company undertook a training exercise dealing mainly with strategic aspects for a large government department employing about 35 purchasing staff. During early discussions when we asked for a breakdown of the annual spends they were unable to supply it because they had an inadequate computer system.

A finger in the air estimate was in excess of £30 million, but they were installing a new system to gather information that would be operational by the time we ran the course. Come the day of the course the candidates reported that the new system was worse than the old and they had even less information. In addition when we raised the subject of negotiation we were told that the subject was irrelevant to them 'as they always sent out for three or more quotes and always accepted the cheapest – they never undertook any negotiation'. In profit and loss terms they must have been making a thumping great loss and if they had been employed in much of the private sector they would not have held onto their jobs for very long. A warning therefore to purchasing management who are unsure what weaknesses the system will expose: it is better to thoroughly test it in private before even beginning to mention it outside your department. Better keep quiet, hang onto your job and gain time to correct the flaws that will be exposed.

Chapter summary

A profit and loss measurement system:

- Provides a tool to measure department and team performance.

- Uses an accepted financial format.

- Is credible to the whole organization.

- Builds business within a business concepts.

- Can expose inefficient loss-making departments.

CHAPTER 4

MEASURING AND IMPROVING BUYER PERFORMANCE

THE PROGRAMME

Right away no one is pretending that assessing how well individual Purchasing staff are doing their jobs and presenting their contribution in an objective credible format is an easy task. However, the relationship of purchasing to the financial health of the organization is an opportunity that all too often we do not choose to exploit to maximum potential.

A comprehensive step by step programme that builds on the basics is therefore required to change the situation. In this chapter we focus on the performance measurement and development of individuals rather than the whole department or teams as outlined in the previous chapter. However, it is essential that the recommended Profit & Loss Purchasing Measurement System (Chapter 3) is employed in conjunction with the individual measures described in this chapter as a complete unified package.

THE PEOPLE PERFORMANCE MEASUREMENT PROGRAMME

The complete package as a comprehensive step-by-step programme consists of:

1. dynamic job descriptions
2. key competency assessment
3. training needs analysis
4. performance appraisals and objectives setting

Each of these is discussed overleaf.

1.   Dynamic job descriptions (JDs)

Modern business practice dictates that JDs are the foundation on which to build all people performance measurement programmes. One of the problems about job descriptions, however, is that they are often considered to be another piece of administrative bureaucracy: everyone plays lip service to them but they often lie in the file for years without being dusted down, reconsidered and more importantly used. Bear in mind therefore that they must be very carefully considered in the first place and subsequently regularly revisited and amended to reflect the business environment as it changes and evolves.

Let's go back to the basis of creating them: firstly and most importantly, bear in mind that a job description must be just that – it is all about how the job should best be done *not* about the individual who may just happen to currently fill the post. Properly drawn up and managed they are a very effective communication tool to obtain commitment from people. They lay the very foundation stone to make people accountable for their actions that are judged by being measured against mutually agreed criteria. It is now fashionable, and certainly it possesses some merit, for individuals to draw up their own job descriptions. OK maybe as a first draft – but detailed, clearly defined guidelines must first be in place, otherwise let us charitably describe them as 'mischief making' individuals can drive a coach and horses through the consultative process. However, whatever method is chosen for producing job descriptions, consultation must be the name of the game as commitment can only be obtained with involvement and genuine agreement between jobholders and management. They also need to be formally signed off by both parties and held securely on their personnel files.

Generically, job descriptions should carry the following information:

- job title;
- location (department, business unit, section and so on);
- reporting line including direct accountability and dotted line (always include an organization chart);
- direct reports – jobs reporting directly to the job holder;
- primary purpose of job (ideally one line or a very short paragraph);
- key responsibilities and accountabilities (listed as numbered points);
- dimensions (job content, scope of the position together with secondary duties);

- working arrangements (for example, need for overtime working or call-outs)
- decision-making responsibilities and procedures to be followed;
- essential and desirable qualifications, knowledge and experience;
- ethical guidelines;
- job contacts and business relationships.

By far the most difficult section to describe and write is the *key responsibilities* section. A good way of producing the required eight to fifteen key responsibilities of a job is to:

1. Brainstorm in a completely random fashion a list of the most important and crucial aspects of the job.
2. Carefully consider responsibilities such as expenditure limits, decision making, planning, negotiating, expediting, monitoring, reporting processes, communicating with and managing people internally and at suppliers, inputs, outputs and so on.
3. Now combine, develop and edit the random collection of ideas into a set of essential key responsibilities. A junior position should not require more than eight and even the most senior position should not require more than fifteen.
4. Rank them in order of importance.
5. Obtain a second opinion from somebody who knows the job well.
6. Revisit and carefully consider that all the key responsibilities are really important, fair and achievable for every individual possessing the competencies to fill the position.

Avoid having a key responsibility as vague or imprecise as 'Always keep our internal customers happy'.

Coincidentally, this section is the most important part from the subsequent performance measurement point of view; therefore it is vital that this list is succinct and complete. It is also utterly pointless just listing a responsibility without also saying how it is expected to be tackled to achieve success.

An example of one key responsibility for a Senior Buyer is as follows:

- *Produce and maintain a best-in-class supplier portfolio for furniture products.*

OK – but how do they go about it? Tell them therefore how they are expected to achieve the task by adding the methodology.

- *Produce and maintain a best-in-class supplier portfolio for furniture products. By persuading internal customers to always accept our approved standard range of desks and chairs for all replacements and new items. By employing the supplier evaluation system to ensure that only A or B rated suppliers are ever used. By formally reviewing and reporting on at least 45 per cent of the supplier base each year, researching new suppliers for problem areas and by seeking innovative solutions.*

Do not forget to regularly review and revise job descriptions to ensure that they stay in line with the changes that affect the methods of working that are always taking place in most organizations.

2.   Key competencies

The job description will clarify what the job consists of, what needs to be done and the responsibilities that the post carries. We now need to decide the qualities that should be possessed by the current jobholder or candidates for a new position to be able to carry out the work as specified to a very high standard. A good way to do this is to draw up a list of key competencies that people need to possess in order to be able to do the job effectively.

Job competency profiles will help to assess:

- Can the person do the job effectively? Do they have the knowledge, skills and experience to perform well?
- Does the person possess the right personal qualities required to be able to do the job? Can they do it, do they really want to do it or are they just a square peg in a round hole?
- How does the person do the job? Do they fit well into the organization? Do colleagues and suppliers respect them and do they generally work well in a team?

Above all, the advantages of establishing a comprehensive and carefully considered competency framework for each job, or series of jobs, is that it effectively removes the subjectivity that is part of the human emotional frailty of us all when we make a personal judgement of others. It is well known that we form subconscious opinions within seconds of meeting someone and presumably we have all experienced the exciting meeting of eyes across a crowded room! Great in a social setting but hardly the basis for making decisions about people in the workplace. (See Chapter 11 – Body Language.) With the right competency framework and an unbiased scoring system, common ground can be established to talk to people objectively, even about sensitive issues like the personality traits they display when they are doing their job.

A Competency Framework can be designed around two main headings:

- non-technical competencies
- technical competencies.

Non-technical competencies
These are generally non-job-specific skills and should include:

1. Working with other people
- managing relationships
- team working
- influencing
- leadership.

2. Working with information
- gathering and analysing information
- decision making.

3. Future development
- personal development of self and others
- innovation and generating new ideas
- managing change.

4. Delivering results
- planning and organizing
- operational management
- objective setting
- customer service.

Each of these categories is described in more detail overleaf.

1. Working with other people
Managing relationships
Realizes the need for opening, developing and maintaining healthy professional relationships conducive to getting the job done well. Is sensitive
to the views of others and continually nourishes and grows good working
relationships at all levels both internally and externally. Treats suppliers as
equals and is considered to be firm but fair by the majority. Is generally
regarded as being trustworthy, flexible and approachable by internal
customers and can be relied upon to deliver their requirements promptly and
efficiently.

Team working
Displays a preference for working in teams and is happy to acknowledge
that team working produces results far outweighing the sum of the individual
member contribution. Is good at building, and if necessary leading, effective
teams (sometimes cross-functional) who produce results that meet the
organization's objectives promptly and economically. Adopts a friendly
and open approach which puts other team members at ease and builds
their confidence. Sensitive to possible conflicts as they surface and works
to negate them and promote harmony. Sets an example of remaining calm
under pressure and always strives for the team to make objective decisions
based on the available facts.

Influencing
Gains the respect of others by being professional and knowledgeable of the
subject. Articulate and self-confident, able to present ideas cogently to an
individual or in front of a group. Is a very good communicator who can win
over the acceptance of doubters by the force of logical argument without
arousing resentment. Is a sensitive listener who acknowledges the views of
others without being diverted from gaining their acceptance and support for
own opinions. Is highly motivated and skilled at persuading others to see his
or her own point of view.

Leadership
Has that certain presence that makes them able to influence a group by quickly
winning their respect and admiration. Is strong minded but still willing to
listen to the opinions of others and works hard at making all members of
the group feel included and valued whilst still giving the impression of not
suffering fools gladly. Is happy and confident to lead and accept responsibility.
Is decisive and able to focus on the real issues. Driven to achieve results by

being good at managing, organizing and delegating. A good leader is friendly but not overfriendly, standing very slightly aloof from the crowd, never expressing fear nor favour to anyone.

2. Working with information
Gathering and analysing information
Makes objective decisions based on facts, not on subjective emotions or feelings. Gathers, organizes and presents information logically so that others can easily appreciate its relevance. Skilled at analysing complex data with an ability to select the meaningful issues that need consideration whilst not getting mired in too much detail. Possesses good computer skills such as employing and manipulating spreadsheets to analyse large volumes of complex information. Conclusions and decisions are based on an audit trail of identifiable facts. Highly numerate and articulate.

Decision making
Must be skilled at analysing situations, considering the facts and making timely objective decisions that are always followed through. Maintains an open mind and whilst being sensitive to the opinions of others will not shirk from making difficult decisions when required. Has the confidence to admit a mistake and possesses the flexibility to swiftly make corrective changes. Takes into account the medium- and long-term consequence of decisions carefully weighing the possible risks and has the foresight to institute the right degree of contingency planning. Remains calm and logical in difficult situations and is never panicked into making decisions. Is willing to stand out from the crowd, not following the party line if he or she does not agree with it.

3. Future development
Personal development of self and others
Believes that no one ever stops learning and is always keen to explore new ideas. A generous and supportive mentor always encouraging and helping others to develop and grow their potential both professionally and personally. Carefully targets training to address knowledge gaps effectively to the benefit of the organization and the individual.

Innovation and generating new ideas
A strong advocate of the continuous improvement culture (Kaizen), constantly seeking better ways of doing things. Highly innovative, seen as a go-getting person always keen to pursue and exploit new business

opportunities to benefit the organization. Encourages others to take the same attitude whilst at the same time not forgetting the basics of remaining logical and objective when analysing the merits of new ideas. Does not get carried away with the fashion of change for change's sake but instead plans ways of mitigating risks that may arise.

Managing change

Appreciates the inevitability and benefits of change, and in general will support and drive it forward. However, he or she is willing to question its merits if there are no positive benefits to be achieved. Remains aware that many people are reluctant or even unable to accept change so exceptional leadership and persuasional skills are required to promote major organizational changes by way of continual honest communication at all levels. An ability to stay focused on the objectives is essential to overcome the uncertain, stressful and difficult situations that will always arise.

4.   Delivering results

Planning and organizing

Takes a systematic approach to work ensuring that pertinent information is filed and stored logically in order that it can be quickly retrieved when required. A tidy desk approach is preferable! Prioritizes work continually whilst maintaining the flexibility to rethink to accommodate priority changes that inevitably constantly occur in a fast moving dynamic environment. Manages time to ensure all aspects of the work are covered to schedule. Is able to work effectively under pressure and stay focused on the programme of work. Draws up realistic project plans to cover all aspects of a task and drives it forward by obtaining commitment from colleagues and suppliers. Monitors progress and results, taking corrective action if problems occur. Is aware of organizational strategy ensuring that day-to-day operations and actions do not adversely clash with it. Thrives on problem solving by being quick thinking and practical, never thinking that any crisis is impossible to overcome by one means or another.

Operational management

Develops a reputation for getting things done whatever the circumstances. Is approachable to everyone presenting a practical down-to-earth approach to the task in hand. Maintains that quality and deadlines are sacrosanct, leads by example showing qualities of determination, tenacity and hard work. Thrives on responsibility and solving problems and can quickly adapt to change. Skilled at project management and displays a ruthless streak for completing projects on time, to budget and of high quality. Excellent job knowledge is key to successful operational management and inspires confidence in colleagues and suppliers.

Objective setting
Convinced that the setting of well defined measurable objectives and performance targets are key to success for both self and subordinates. Aware that objectives will not work if imposed and success can only be achieved by gaining agreement and co-operation, is therefore prepared to discuss, consult and compromise if necessary. Medium and long-term objectives must not clash with organizational strategy. Focuses thrust of objectives on continuous improvement and obtaining better value for money.

Customer service
Maintains that 'the customer is king' and that buyers only deserve to keep their jobs if they continue to satisfy their internal customers. Does not suffer maverick buying gladly and is strong on marketing and selling professional purchasing expertise. Strives always to supply a high quality, cost-effective service to the organization. Promotes a culture of excellence being the norm.

Technical competencies
These may incorporate job specific requirements that can usually be included within the following headings:

1. Strategic procurement
    *   procurement strategy
    *   assessment of specifications and customer requirements
    *   supplier sourcing and evaluation
    *   negotiation planning
    *   IT Systems. Awareness of the possibilities and potential of computerization.

2. Operational procurement
    *   enquiry processing
    *   contract management
    *   negotiation
    *   order placing and expediting
    *   supplier management and development
    *   departmental management.

3. Additional specialist technical competencies
   - IT skills
   - logistics skills
   - sales and marketing skills
   - finance and accounting skills
   - legal knowledge
   - other skills that are relevant to the job.

Each of these categories is described in more detail below.

1. Strategic procurement

Procurement strategy

In line with the requirements of the job, maintains a current knowledge of the global economic and political climate as it affects the organization in general and in particular the supply marketplace for the products and services covering their sphere of responsibility. This may include such items as legal and regulatory changes, competition, cartels, global raw material shortfall, supplier mergers and other general financial and supply chain threats. Is acknowledged by the organization as being an expert in the field and is therefore listened to and consulted when organizational strategy is being discussed. Supplies an early warning and problem-solving system when outside influences emerge as a potential threat to business strategy. Is therefore knowledgeable on the entire supply chain including, for example, logistics, raw materials, second and third tier supplier marketplaces. By effective communication and persuasion constantly promotes the strategic benefits of best practice procurement throughout the organization. Possesses the ability to strategically analyse and segment the commodity portfolio and take the required action to secure supply and allocate resources to the areas of greatest return or high level concern.

Assessment of specifications and customer requirements

Maintains excellent relationships with peer group internal customers to keep abreast of their changing requirements and is therefore appreciated for making a valuable team contribution at the planning and specification preparation stages. Possesses business and technical expertise of the operating marketplaces and brings it to bear in guiding internal customers to adopt cost-effective solutions without compromising the required quality levels. Ensures that specifications are clear and unambiguous in order that suppliers do not misunderstand them.

Supplier sourcing and evaluation
Employs skills and experience to investigate, analyse and source from the marketplace, either local or global, bearing in mind the strategic implications. Plays a role in formulating and employing the organization's objective procedures for supplier evaluation and selection. Measures supplier performance on an ongoing basis and is an advocate of supplier improvement programmes. Is skilled at risk assessment.

Negotiation planning
Realizes that the amount of effort expended on the preparatory work is directly proportional to the achievement of a successful outcome. Adopts a pragmatic tactical approach to negotiation planning by careful analysis to predict the key objectives of both parties and by definition the likely sticking points in the negotiation. Plans affordable concessions to overcome objections to obtain own key objectives. Decides ahead on the minimum acceptable result and will walk away to fight another day rather than accept a lesser offer.

IT systems. Awareness of the possibilities and potential of computerization
Whilst not necessarily being a technical computer expert maintains a watching brief on IT developments and the benefits that they may bring. Possesses therefore a broad knowledge of the advantages and disadvantages of modern IT, for example, reverse auctions (see Chapter 12), materials requirement planning (MRP), enterprise resource planning (ERP) and so on to aid procurement and supply chain management. Promotes the advantages of fully integrated systems for streamlining processes and, for instance, eliminating double keying, thereby reducing human error. Procurement is a major user of IT and must therefore play a defining role in specifying and planning the organization's computerization programmes.

2. Operational procurement
Enquiry processing
Experienced at an operational practical level of dealing with the handling of the procedures involved in procurement sourcing covering requests for information (RFIs), invitations to tender (ITTs), devising selection criteria, evaluation of bids and so on.

Contract management
Is aware of the importance of drawing up effective contracts from the point of view of good communication and protecting the organization contractually. Very wary of the legal pitfalls and implications that a badly drawn up contract can incur. Undertakes regular contract reviews in conjunction with internal customers and suppliers, instigates corrective action when required.

Negotiation
Is a skilled, resourceful and effective negotiator who commands the respect of suppliers. Likes winning and can turn on the right negotiating style to suit the occasion – chameleon like! Adopts a very shrewd commercial approach, prepares well and is always very determined to succeed. Negotiation with internal customers that may require a more conciliatory and diplomatic approach is also an important skill set that should not be neglected.

Order placing and expediting
Organizes and promptly reacts to automatic stock replenishment systems or requests from internal customers. Reviews reorder triggers in line with the lead times that are available from the marketplace. Uses the available IT such as MRP systems to minimize on shelf stock whilst maximizing availability. Solves problems connected with late delivery with effective expediting procedures. Takes the entire supply chain into consideration including transport, logistics, materials handling, raw materials, secondary suppliers, shipping, import administration and so on.

Supplier management and development
Realizes that establishing and managing supplier relationships is absolutely key to the procurement process. Accepts responsibility for instigating and maintaining excellent communication channels ensuring that instructions in contracts and purchase orders are clear and unambiguous. Always treats suppliers firmly but fairly and exhibits neither fear nor favour to any. Insists that suppliers report any supply or quality problems promptly and not bury their heads in the sand up to the point of late delivery. Installs reliable supplier measurement procedures and for key commodities devises mutually beneficial supplier continuous improvement programmes.

Departmental management (Can also be applied to team or section management)
Possesses the appropriate level of purchasing management experience to be able to lead by example. Is good at gaining the confidence of colleagues so

that they accept responsibility for work that is delegated to them. Is a trusted and popular mentor in developing staff to achieve their true potential. Works enthusiastically at promoting a culture of professionalism and efficiency in all purchasing matters and takes every opportunity of marketing and selling this expertise throughout the organization and to the supply side. Is considered by peers to be the commercial expert to consult on all procurement matters that affect the organization.

3. Additional specialist technical competencies

These definitions are very dependent on the requirement of individual organizations or specific jobs and are only offered to stimulate the consideration of special circumstances.

IT skills

May demand a knowledge of the computer systems sufficient to be the department expert and therefore provide the communication link to the IT Department (or external supplier) and be able to solve day-to-day operational computer problems as they occur. Is very confident and comfortable at operating the PC software that they are expected to operate. Uses PC expertise, for example Excel spreadsheets, to effectively assist in analysing large amounts of data. Has the knowledge to use computer systems innovatively and creatively to advantage.

Logistics skills

Appreciates and takes into account the importance of materials flow, transport and distribution to the efficient working of the supply chain. Depending on the commodities purchased, MRP systems skills may also be required.

Sales and marketing skills

Often a neglected area within the purchasing profession that this book seeks to address – see Chapters 6 to 11.

Finance and accounting skills

A vital area for purchasing professionals to be proficient in as we should be able to speak the same language as accountants if we are going to make the organization realize our important contribution to its financial health. Job training exchanges with the Finance Department are often mutually beneficial.

Legal knowledge
Buyers really do need sufficient knowledge of contract law to protect the
organization when setting up deals with suppliers. This knowledge should also
extend to an appreciation of when is the appropriate time to seek the advice
of legal professionals if matters are becoming beyond their expertise.

3.   Training needs analysis

All too often weak or inexperienced management dish out training courses
in the same way that children are rewarded with sweets for good behaviour.
However, this is the point where enlightened management really starts to
benefit from the hard work put into steps 1 and 2 of the programme. Using
effective *job descriptions* and *key competency analysis* it is then relatively
easy to develop a *training needs matrix* using a spreadsheet format to
objectively score the training requirements of each individual. This enables
departmental training to be planned and executed to high standards within
budget.

Competencies	Strategy	Sourcing	Negotiation	Team Management	IT Skills	Legal
Joe Bloggs	7/10	8/10	8/10	4/10	5/10	4/10
Mary Smith	4/10	7/10	7/10	8/10	6/10	4/10
Fred Jones	6/10	8/10	4/10	7/10	7/10	4/10

Figure 4.1   Example of a training needs matrix

The example above is obviously an oversimplified version of the spreadsheet
layout that is required but nevertheless shows a simple scoring system can be
used to assess individual strengths and weaknesses against job descriptions
and key competencies. In this instance Joe's people skills are weak and need
addressing via perhaps an external course and by regular review. Similarly
Mary needs help on the appreciation of strategy and Fred on negotiating
skills. They all appear to have gaps in their legal knowledge so perhaps
an internal course for the whole department would provide the most cost-
effective solution.

It is very important to draw up a training needs matrix in conjunction
with staff by agreeing on the scoring and consequently the areas that need
development.

It is as well to consider all the means of delivering training that are available. External training courses are good from the usefulness of meeting other buyers from a wide range of businesses and organizations but they are restricted when it comes to addressing individual problems. In-house courses are better in this respect as they can combine training with an element of consultancy advice to solve specific problems. They can also be cheaper if there are sufficient candidates to attend. Job exchanges within the organization can also be very effective, for instance with departments such as Finance, Sales and Marketing. Computer based training will suit some people. Of course on the job training goes on all the time and it is sometimes advantageous to formalise this with a mentoring programme.

4.   Performance appraisals and objective setting

Even in cases where an organization does not have a formal appraisal system it is strongly recommended that the Purchasing Department introduce one, as it is an ideal vehicle for improving purchasing performance. Appraisals benefit both management and staff by improving job performance and by objectively identifying strengths and weaknesses. They also help to plan training and development programmes, employing of course a training needs matrix. They are used to review both past performance and future potential. They can also be linked to reward review. Their format is a fairly formal interview/discussion between each member of staff and their immediate manager. It is arranged as a 'tablets of stone' appointment with at least one month's notice being given. They should take place at least twice a year with regular key performance monitoring in between.

Purchasing is an ideal area for management by objectives (MBO) as clear objectives can be introduced and regularly monitored. An objective for a buyer might be 'a reduction of 8 per cent on average will be obtained in the next twelve months across the range of commodity spend responsibility'. An objective like this can be seen as clear, unambiguous and easy to measure. This is the type of objective that can be linked to the Profit & Loss Procurement Measurement System for instance, to show when an individual is not performing as well as the rest of the team. About five or six key objectives should be agreed. Objectives therefore need to be clear, agreed, achievable, measurable, regularly monitored and supported by management. Do not set people up to fail.

Written records by the manager of the appraisals meetings are essential to provide feedback to both staff members and senior management: they are used to display progress or lack of it. Managers and staff members must agree and sign off the appraisal record. In the case of dispute an arbitration procedure should also be in place. An appraisal in a purchasing environment is used principally to monitor actual job performance and rate it against agreed objectives. Overall performance ratings can be given as follows:

1. Outstanding
2. Exceeded requirements
3. Meets requirements
4. Shows minor weaknesses
5. Shows significant weaknesses
6. Unacceptable.

Obviously if a manager is of the opinion that a staff member should be marked as 4, 5, or 6 on the above scale, they should have strong evidence to be able to prove it to the staff member, senior management and human resources. It is a sign of management weakness if most ratings are gathered around the median point because it is demotivating to above-average performers and it lets sub-standard performers off the hook.

An appraisal records checklist might look as follows:

1.   Personal details – name, department, length of time in job and so on
2.   Job title
3.   Job description
4.   Training record
5.   Review of performance against objectives and other job-related criteria
6.   New or revised objectives
7.   Performance rating against objectives plus a general performance rating
8.   Comments by a more senior manager
9.   Comments by staff member
10. Training and development plan
11. Signing off to signify agreement by staff member, immediate manager and a more senior manager

Commitment by all parties is essential because merely paying lip service to appraisal schemes can be motivationally disastrous and damage morale hugely. It is probably one of the most important tasks of all for management to perform as staff need to be appreciated to deliver excellence and therefore deserve regular amounts of quality uninterrupted time with a listening manager.

Chapter summary

- People performance measurement comes as a package.

- Job descriptions are the important first step.

- Produce key competency requirements for each job.

- Plan training using a skills gap matrix.

- Employ regular formal appraisals using management by objectives measures of individual performance and to high-light development needs.

CHAPTER 5

MEASURING SUPPLIER PERFORMANCE

THE SCOPE FOR MEASUREMENT

There is one incident that is indelibly etched in my memory of the time when I realized that as a manager I really must do something about better measuring supplier performance in a much more comprehensive manner, to include soft as well as hard measures. To provide some background to the moment of my wake-up call, the incident concerns the direct mail team at Abbey National, a bunch of experienced, very technically proficient buyers whom as their senior manager I was rightly proud of. Direct mail had been outsourced a few years previously to an industry that was quite unprepared to handle the rigours of financial services mailings. Up until then direct mail production companies had been mainly confined to sending out commercial items such as sales letters or money-off coupons because bank and building societies organized their own direct mail production in-house. In this context it did not matter too much if envelopes arrived unsealed or contained either none or five money-off coupons. However, Abbey National customers would go ballistic if they opened their mail expecting to see a personal mortgage statement only to find the sealed envelope empty, while worse still their next-door neighbour received two statements, including their neighbour's missing one. They also were also quite rightly annoyed if the envelope were not properly sealed because there was a danger that other people would have access to their personal financial information. We had therefore been forced to devise, pioneer and impose a whole range of quality control and assurance systems on the companies that we had outsourced to. These changes consisted of in-depth statistical sampling, better controls and the invention of more sophisticated equipment. Some mailings were very large at around four million, therefore if we received a customer complaint it could have gone wrong at one of several suppliers – either data preparation or mailing production companies. But by using a unique sequential number we could identify exactly where and when things had gone wrong. We would know which company, which machine, which operator, the time produced, the time supplied to the Royal Mail and finally we were able to check the retained statistical samples from before and after the faulty example. As an example of the depth of detail involved, if an unsealed envelope complaint was received, we would even know when the operator had last checked the level of the water bottle reservoir on the enveloping machine.

I knew therefore that our quality control was state of the art and we had hard evidence on the suppliers that were supplying the best quality on time. However, returning to my wake-up call mentioned in the opening paragraph, the buyers were forming their opinions of suppliers based on a completely different set of subjective criteria of their own individual creation. When questioned, they would list items such as responsiveness, quality of account handling, flexibility, availability of sales reps, prompt answering of the telephone, co-operation with the Royal Mail, documentation, cultural clash and so on. Although in the main the criticisms were not show stoppers, they did affect the way that buyers did their jobs. Let us call these criteria the soft measures and unless tackled will often remain highly subjective. For instance, one buyer would say that a certain supplier takes ages to answer the phone while another would say that they never have any trouble.

THE ANSWER – A COMPREHENSIVE SUPPLIER EVALUATION, ACCREDITATION AND RATING SYSTEM

Many supplier rating or vendor rating systems, especially of the computerized variety, measure only the hard information items such as late delivery measured in hours or quality defects per thousand. My wake-up call had, however, confirmed that this was only half the story: we also needed the soft measures, plus more team people involvement to bring another dimension to the pages of statistics and graphs. However, once the work was started it was soon obvious that supplier rating was only part of the process: it was also essential to install a supplier evaluation and accreditation system to generate a cultural revaluation of how we should ideally be choosing, measuring and treating our suppliers.

HANDLING SUPPLIERS

A supplier portfolio should be treated as a valuable asset in the same way that a portfolio of share investments is cherished. A wise investor will constantly monitor the stock market and his share portfolio to check which high performing assets, by way of dividend return and capital appreciation, are retained and which poor performers are to be disposed of at the first favourable opportunity. All too often, however, buyers will treat suppliers, especially potential new suppliers with contempt and disdain. Power seems to go completely to the heads of some, and I should know, as for the past few years I have been running my own business trying to sell procurement consultancy, recruitment and training. Some inexperienced buyers have closed minds because in their opinion they already know it all. It is a pity that they do not realize that to be truly professional they should treat suppliers in the same manner as they would like to be treated themselves. After all, suppliers as well as buyers can choose whom they deal with. Word gets around quickly and the best suppliers choose the customers that treat them fairly and ignore the rest. Rude and arrogant buyers get the inefficient suppliers that they deserve. (See Chapter 10 – Reverse Marketing.)

However, as well as measuring supplier performance we need to ensure that we have discovered the best available suppliers in the first place.

THE SUPPLIER PORTFOLIO DILEMMA

Good practice dictates that a small supplier portfolio is maintained and most organizations have been working hard over the past few years to reduce their supplier base. Lazy buyers can use this as an excuse to brush off the consideration of new suppliers. However, in a fast moving world, to maintain a best-in-class portfolio, professional buyers will always be on the lookout for new suppliers that are developing faster than others. The dilemma of limiting the size of the supplier portfolio whilst still being on the lookout for new ones can be managed by employing an efficient supplier evaluation and accreditation system.

SUPPLIER EVALUATION AND ACCREDITATION

The objective of a supplier evaluation and accreditation system must be to maintain a portfolio of best-in-class suppliers by ensuring that the changes constantly occurring in the marketplace are taken into account and acted upon. This is achieved by maintaining an open door policy, treating all potential suppliers fairly and demonstrating professionalism by supplying positive unbiased feedback based on factual and measurable requirements. The process need not be overly time-consuming if procedures are in place to automate the process as much as possible. It is suggested that any accreditation and evaluation system be introduced gradually by concentrating initially on the most strategically important commodities. Inevitably it never needs to be introduced for the 'paper clip' type suppliers because the time taken on low spend unimportant commodities cannot usually be justified.

For most purchases the common areas that need consideration can be broadly split into three areas that can be graded according to the information obtained from the evaluation and accreditation process:

A. Financial status – including, for example, financial strength, costing and reporting systems, track record, profitable growth, inventory management, assets, blue chip customer portfolio.

B. Quality and environment – including, for example, quality assurance system, quality accreditations, quality manuals, environmental standards. You may also want to rate supplier ethical policies if your company operates a strict ethical code. (See Chapter 13.)

C. Equipment, technology, premises, culture – including, for example, up to date kit, modern premises, efficient workflow, IT systems employed, distribution methods, people attitudes and enlightened management standards, approved second and third tier suppliers.

A working model is now listed to demonstrate the technique and suggest the individual areas that should be considered. Of course the model will need adjusting to suit your organization and the commodities being purchased. Also the values to be applied and measured will vary according to circumstances. For instance, under 'Financial status' you will need to decide how long a company should have been in business to be described as 'well established' or how you should value 'strong working capital' – maybe as a ratio to turnover? A tame accountant comes in useful at this stage!

A. Financial status

Grade one supplier
- well established company
- strong working capital
- substantial net worth
- continual profitable growth
- effective cost controls.

Grade two supplier
- well established company
- positive working capital
- positive net worth
- maintained growth
- profits and borrowing remain at satisfactory levels
- remains fundamentally strong despite slight performance drop during one or two of the past financial years.

Grade three supplier
- working capital and cash flow resources depleted
- increased reliance on bank borrowings and/or external funding
- negative net worth
- sustained losses
- displays weak working capital and cash flow positions.

Grade four supplier
- company is suffering from a deficit of working capital
- unacceptable losses sustained
- failure to file audited accounts on time.

B. Quality

Grade one supplier
- ISO corporate registration for quality standards in place
- displays high-level commitment to environmental standards.

Grade two supplier
- quality systems in place that broadly meet the required ISO standards
- is well into the process of obtaining ISO accreditation
- meets some of the environmental standards.

Grade three supplier
- quality manuals in place
- documented working procedures
- quality assurance processes in operation
- regular quality audits take place
- realizes the importance of environmental standards.

Grade four supplier
- does not think ISO standards are relevant
- has no quality improvement programmes in place
- ignores environmental standards.

C. Equipment, technology, premises, culture

Grade one supplier
- has a range of modern, state-of-the-art, high-tech equipment housed in up-to-date premises
- possesses the experience, high capacity and capability to produce all the services required
- excellent planned maintenance and reliable contingency arrangements in place
- efficient workflow and excellent housekeeping displayed
- is an acknowledged market leader with a track record of innovation.

Grade two supplier
- able to offer a good range of the services required. A mix of new and old equipment
- offers medium capacity
- good preventive maintenance with some contingency arrangements in place
- good housekeeping and workflow
- displays commitment to technological change
- perhaps an up-and-coming business.

Grade three supplier
- able to offer some of the services required
- equipment not the latest
- untidy premises with poor housekeeping
- limited capacity/volume
- maintenance if and when required
- not state-of-the-art technologically.

Grade four supplier
- new business, not well established in the marketplace
- or established, old fashioned, poorly equipped company
- does not display the expertise required.

Whilst the methodology should remain common, not all commodities will require grade one suppliers, so a minimum standard will need to be drawn up for each commodity purchased. This process will require careful managing as it will be perfectly natural for buyers to think that all the commodities they are responsible for are very important and therefore require their suppliers to be graded one for everything. Reference to the strategic analysis Boston matrix in Chapter 2 page 19 will prove invaluable in sorting out disputes.

EVALUATION AND ACCREDITATION PROCEDURES

So a new company approaches the buying department offering to provide a superior service to the one that is currently purchased. They could be told to get lost, but it is far better to take a professional approach using a set of easily adopted procedures. After all, your company may not need them now but will in the future, or think about looking after your own interests:. you may change job and discover that they are a vital supplier to your new employer.

It is also very important for the organization to present a professional and consistent face to the marketplace, especially when several buyers are involved. Procedures are required to ensure that both the organization and its buyers treat all suppliers, both existing and potential, 'in the way that we would like to be treated ourselves'. No apologies for mentioning this truism several times in this book!

Later the importance of reverse marketing is discussed. (See Chapter 10.) By adopting a set of procedures that demonstrably exhibit a fair and open approach to evaluating and adopting new suppliers, reverse marketing good practice becomes ingrained.

A sample set of supplier evaluation and accreditation procedures is included in Appendix 1 (page 151) that can quickly be adapted and customized to suit any organizational requirement.

SUPPLIER RATING

A supplier rating (sometimes called vendor rating) system complements the evaluation and accreditation system in that it measures the performance of approved suppliers on an ongoing basis and supplies meaningful feedback in order to improve performance. In the opening to this chapter I mentioned that buyers could sometimes be very subjective when judging suppliers; therefore, the goal of any rating system must be the application of consistent objective criteria to measuring and reporting performance.

During my career in purchasing management over the years I tried to introduce several different supplier rating systems with varying degrees of success. Upon reflection I realized that they did not work that well because they tended to be used mainly as an internal departmental tool which was wheeled out occasionally to beat a supplier about the head with. My 'eureka' moment came with the revelation that any rating system must be completely open to all. This means that any piece of information or opinion that a buyer uses to judge a supplier is not valid or acceptable unless the buyer is prepared to sit across the table and tell the supplier face to face any concerns they have that may affect the supplier adversely. Plus if necessary the supplier can appeal to purchasing management if the findings are not fair by way of perhaps gross inaccuracy or sheer subjectivity. Buyers must learn to 'put their money where their mouth is' and if they wish to criticize or indeed praise suppliers they must be prepared to tell suppliers like it is and be able to back it up, not just moan to their mates around the photocopier.

To be effective any supplier rating system must therefore be fair, consistent measurable and objective. The findings of the system must be reported on a regular basis preferably on a face-to-face basis with the application of a culture that any shortcomings revealed should be corrected by both buyer and supplier working together to achieve solutions. Of course, when things go badly wrong and no improvements are in sight, there will come a time to drop a supplier, but at least there will be a clear audit trail to show the supplier where they have gone wrong and why they have been dropped.

It is almost a given that any rating system should be based on the three good old favourites *price, quality* and *service*. The system that this book demonstrates is based on absolute perfection being given a score of 100 with points being deducted when perfection is not achieved. The way that the total 100 points score is allocated to either price, quality or service will vary by product grouping. For instance, on some ranges of products, quality and service may be far more important than price so perhaps on these quality will have a maximum score of 50, service a score of 40 and price a score of 10 to form the total 100 score. Measuring is carried out on an order by order, buyer by buyer basis for each commodity grouping. The scores are accumulated and reported internally on a monthly basis. At the start of each month all suppliers start with a clean slate score of 100 and points are then deducted as work is delivered where performance has not met the required standards. Depending on the points total, suppliers will receive a consolidated rating of either A, B, C or D with obviously A being the highest. Where there are several buyers working in the same commodity grouping a monthly team meeting must be held to reach consensus on the consolidated rating for each supplier. The buyers then must all sing from the same hymn sheet when talking to suppliers and internal customers about performance ratings; the old individual subjective opinions must be relegated to the scrap heap.

Consolidated scores are fed back to suppliers, usually on a quarterly basis, by a face-to-face, across the table meeting preferably between a senior person from the supplier with the authority to instigate change and someone of similar standing from Purchasing. Exceptions to this quarterly meeting timetable may be required if drastic problems occur in one month and immediate action is essential, or to the contrary when a very efficient supplier produces consistently high level scores, perhaps only half-yearly meetings will be required. It may also be wise to have monthly reporting meetings with newly accredited suppliers.

Supplier rating measurement criteria

Scoring may be based on the following criteria:

Price
- marketplace competitiveness
- discounts and payment terms offered
- flexibility
- estimate – timeliness and accuracy.

Quality
- zero defects
- on-time delivery
- specifications met
- all-round quality of products and services received

- complaints made
- complaint handling
- presentation (for example, palletization and goods received notes).

Service
- responsiveness (for example, representative availability, telephone answering and so on)
- scheduling and progress reporting
- flexibility
- communication efficiency – oral, written, computer.
- report and paperwork accuracy
- administration efficiency.

PROCEDURES

See Appendix 2 (page 165) for a sample set of procedures.

HOW RATINGS SYSTEMS WORK IN PRACTICE

The second paragraph of this chapter mentions a possible problem with telephone answering response time. Without a ratings system a buyer would mention to a representative that they were not happy with the speed that, say, the production office took to answer their phones. If no one else had complained the representative would not have very much to go on so would probably mention it in passing to the production manager and the chances are that it would be ignored. However, if poor telephone response times became a ratings issue under '*Service* – responsiveness', buyers would quickly decide to measure it by each one deciding to tick a monthly spreadsheet counting the number of rings before the telephone was answered by the supplier's production office. Armed with this chapter and verse evidence and the news that the company had lost their A rating for service, because of production office inefficiency, the supplier would quickly ensure that matters were improved.

SUPPLIER OF THE YEAR AWARDS

This is the next logical step to recognize the efforts and achievements over a twelve-month period of the best suppliers in the portfolio. When visiting suppliers I have always found it remarkable that they take so much pride and pleasure in receiving awards even if they only normally consist of a signed certificate. They are usually carefully framed and hang in a prominent position in the company's reception for all and sundry to admire. Perhaps they are valued so highly because suppliers are more accustomed to receiving brickbats?

The usual format is to issue supplier of the year gold, silver and bronze award certificates for each product category. In each category obviously the company with the highest rating and most points for the year wins the gold award. Other formats can also be considered such as 'best new supplier of the year or champion all-round supplier of the year'.

Presentations of supplier awards offer superb reverse marketing opportunities and these should be made the most of. For instance, you may persuade your managing director or some senior internal customer to present the award certificate to your supplier's managing director. This can then provide public relations opportunities for both organizations by perhaps also asking the local media or dignitaries along to the presentation. Everyone benefits – not least the increasing prestige of Purchasing – by their display of expertise and for organizing matters so well!

It is amazing the lengths in terms of effort and making sure that every detail is right that suppliers will put in to achieve an award from a valued customer. This is just one demonstration of the huge extra benefit that a ratings system can confer on a purchasing organization by way of obtaining better results than buyers from their competition.

SUPPLIER CONFERENCES

A very effective way to make an impact on the supply chain is to hold annual supplier conferences on topical issues. Supplier conferences can also be used as an appropriate opportunity to present supplier awards.

OBTAINING THE COMMITMENT AND TRUST OF SUPPLIERS

Like everyone else, suppliers are often wary of change and the introduction of radical new accreditation and rating systems can frighten some. It is therefore important to carefully consider the sales and marketing effort required to obtain their commitment and co-operation. One way is to produce a comprehensive booklet that carefully explains the new systems and seeks to overcome likely objections. Presentations should also be made and these can be used to provide an added opportunity to develop and hone buyer skills in the public speaking arena. It is very important at an early stage to concentrate on the sales and marketing material. It must look professional even to your supplier's hard-bitten sales director.

So what is in it for suppliers? Well the booklet can point out that accreditation brings benefits in that it is a two-way process for increasing understanding by laying down clearly defined standards for what is expected of a supplier. In addition becoming an accredited supplier means that they can expect the stability of a longer-term relationship.

Supplier ratings actually cement long-term relationships by sharing performance measures with the objective of everybody continuously improving their performance. The supplier will receive regular objective unbiased feedback on their strengths and weaknesses from professional buyers who wish to see them succeed. This will also help them with their other customers because continuous improvement can only enhance their reputation in the marketplace.

Supplier awards recognize top quality service over a sustained period. They are not given lightly because very high standards are expected. However, gaining an award is a concrete recognition of the high regard that the supplier is held in and that they are considered to be a valuable ongoing asset to the business.

A sample set of supplier rating procedures is included in Appendix 2 (page 165) that can quickly be adapted and customized to suit any organizational requirement.

Chapter summary

- Maintaining a best-in-class supplier portfolio is vital.

- An objective and visible evaluation and accreditation system demonstrates that all suppliers are treated fairly.

- Supplier rating systems continually improve all-round performance.

- Supplier conferences and award schemes cement relationships.

CHAPTER 6

MARKETING THEORY

PURCHASING CAN BE ISOLATED WITHIN THE ORGANIZATION

A true story: many years ago I started a new job as deputy to a very experienced Purchasing Manager in Abbey National when it was still a building society and where purchasing was not very high up the pecking order. My manger, Ken Halliford, was a true procurement professional who had plied his trade in the commercial world for many years working for blue chip companies such as Guinness. He became my mentor as he was a superb negotiator, very patient, focused and tenacious and I learned a great deal from watching him operate. However, only my purchasing colleagues and our suppliers realized just what a good job Ken was doing for the organization as he did very little internal networking. When I complained to him that we had no power and were only involved in a tiny proportion of the organization's total spend, his reply invariably was 'Derek, remember we *are* the Purchasing Department and when people need us they know where to find us'. Did they come and find us? Of course not, they were having far too much fun doing their own thing. During our four-year relationship this was the only matter that I ever disagreed with Ken about because even then I instinctively realized that the only way to raise our profile within the organization was to tell our potential internal customers about the skill and expertise we had to offer them.

MARKETING

Many purchasing people are under the mistaken impression that they know all about marketing and selling simply because they regularly do business with sales representatives. However, any buyer who attends a sales course rapidly realizes that they have a tremendous amount to learn. In any case, to approach internal customers with a sales pitch is really putting 'the cart before the horse' because it is unlikely to succeed if no initial marketing has been undertaken. The rule is marketing first, selling second.

The crux of marketing is to find out your customers' real needs and desires and then to create and promote a product or service that fulfils that need and desire. It is proactive NOT a reactive function that requires meaningful research. As well as finding out what makes your target customer really tick, it is also about grabbing their interest and attention, motivating them to buy from you, getting them to make favourable buying decisions and then retaining their business.

It is as well to know something about the basic theory of marketing, even if it is not possible to put it all into practice. However, some elements must be employed in any campaign that aims to achieve success in raising the profile of purchasing within the organization with the objective of winning more business and reducing and eventually eliminating maverick buying. The basic theory boils down to the 5 Ps marketing mix, consisting of *Product, Positioning, Place, Price* and *Promotion.*

PRODUCT

It is absolutely vital that the product or service (the *Product*) being offered is understood from the customers' point of view. There can often be an expectation gap and to be able to manage the minefield of potential misunderstanding all the customers' apprehensions and misconceptions must be appreciated and taken into account.

CUSTOMER EXPECTATIONS	THE GAP	PURCHASING EXPECTATIONS
On demand service Superb response Personal contacts Only we understand our business		Keen prices Professional contracts Objective decisions They need our expertise

A TYPICAL SCENARIO

Figure 6.1   The expectation gap

An important part of managing the expectation gap is to ensure that the *Product* offered has identifiable advantages by way of such items as:

- superior quality
- design benefits
- improved specifications
- better packaging
- reliable guarantees and other lifetime features
- recognizable and memorable branding.

When considering a name for the product, especially one of a technical nature, it is better to concentrate on being more descriptive than creative. In the initial brainstorming session no ideas should be discouraged or rejected no matter how off the wall they may appear to be. As ideas crystallize it is a good idea by common consent to rank them before going on to discuss them in detail and make the final choice. As the final arbiters, the opinions of current and potential customers are vital. International organizations also consult language experts to see that names do not have any unfortunate connotations.

Another subject for brainstorming is the *Product* description. Ideally it should be possible in one concise sentence to explain why the product is perfect for the target market and why it is the best available.

Another *Product* feature to be considered is complexity, as it will not work if the customer does not understand the total package.

POSITIONING

Positioning is defined as what the target customers think about the *Product* offered in relation to competition. In an ideal world it will be viewed as unique and considered to be a benefit by the customers.

There are several *Positioning* strategies to be decided:

- *product* attributes: What specifically does the product offer?
- benefits: What advantages does the *Product* offer?
- users: Identify the potential customer base and who are the decision makers?

- competition: Who are they and what are their strengths and weaknesses?
- differentiation: Identify the *Product's* unique features.

Positioning the *Product* is to attempt to place it in the customers' mind as being special, different and therefore more desirable than the competition. There are several *Positioning* differences that may be considered:

- important: The difference is a valued benefit to the customer;
- distinctive: It has identifiable advantages over the competition;
- superior: Possess visible clear benefits;.
- communicable: Easy to explain and demonstrate the benefits;
- security: Has benefits that the competition cannot easily copy;
- financial: Beneficial to both parties financially.

All this can be distilled down into the *Product Offer* or *Proposition* consisting of the advantages, hopefully unique advantages, which will be explained and promoted to the customers. The *Product Offer* is used by the sales person to grab interest and attention and is the main feature of any advertising and promotional activity. It goes without saying that the *Product Offer* is developed with the customers' interests in mind and is the principal route to satisfying their real needs and wants.

Developing and tailoring the *Product Offer* to suit the customers' needs and wants is key to successfully selling the product or service. There are three main techniques that can be employed to develop the product offer:

1. **FAB: Features, advantages and benefits**. The theory goes that customers do not buy features and they don't even buy advantages – they do buy what the features and advantages will do for them, in sales jargon the benefits. The trick is to come up with the right combination of what the product does and how it does it to present a range of identifiable benefits to the target market or prospect type.

2. **USP: Unique selling points**. This attempts to identify and promote the strongest benefits for a given target market. The problem is that unique to one person is not very special to another. So take two people in the same socio-economic grouping, one living in a suburban house, the other in a city apartment. If someone came to market with a hugely beneficial new gardening product the city

dweller would probably have no need for it, no matter how special it is. It goes to show that allowance must be made for the fact that uniqueness is in the eye of the beholder and their circumstances. USP is a useful sales tool but it may not necessarily provide the right buying trigger.

3. **UPB: Unique perceived benefit**. This is the latest technique to clarify and define the product offer. The problem with FABs and USPs is that they largely address the issue from a sales perspective whereas UPBs have a big advantage because they are a serious attempt to look at the product offer wholly from the customers' viewpoint. It therefore becomes essential that the product offer is a carefully crafted customer orientated presentation. It all comes down to knowing the target market and the individuals that operate in it extremely well. The trick is to firstly identify and then formulate a unique perceived benefit/s package to meet a very carefully researched set of buying motives that has been triggered by the customers' real needs and wants.

Segmentation strategies are also considered under the *Positioning* banner:

- mass marketing, say the whole of the UK, concentrate on common needs and wants rather than regional variations;
- differential marketing is the splitting of the market into segments and producing different offers for each target segment;
- target marketing is to concentrate on a specific slice of the market. This is ideal for testing purposes or for smaller organizations where resources are limited;
- niche marketing is to specialize in a segment that has been ignored or overlooked by the competition.

PLACE

This covers the methods for making the *Product* available to the customer. It may involve the distribution channels, transport and delivery methods, or the geographical locations of functions such as storage or administrative functions. It may also involve policies, procedures and computer systems. *Place* distribution functions can be split into:

- information: Research and information gathering of customer preferences;
- promotion: Communicating the offer to the customer;
- contact: Demonstrating to potential customers;
- matching: Ensuring the product offered matches the buyer's needs and wants;
- negotiation: Agreeing specifications, timing, prices and terms;
- delivery: Supplying the product to the customer;
- finance: Ensuring sufficient funds are available (by both buyer and seller);
- risk: Contingency planning.

PRICE

This is tricky because if the price is too low the offer may be not be taken seriously because it is considered inferior or if the price is too high it may not be taken up because it is thought to be poor value for money. There are various price adjustment methods that can be used to adapt to changing market conditions.

- Discounting: Prices be reduced directly or indirectly to encourage increased customer response such as prompt payment reductions, volume related discounts or annual rebates.
- Discriminatory: Prices may be adjusted to take into account geographical areas or market profile.
- Psychological: For example, make the price £2.99 instead of £3.00. Special sales prices in January or other times when sales mania is being encouraged.
- Value: Use pricing policy to boost the perceived value of the product. The toiletry and perfume market is a good example.
- Promotional: Reduce prices temporarily to boost sales for instance via special offer seasonal promotions.
- Geographical: Adjust prices to take into account the spending power of various locations and the geographical competitive strength.
- International: Price adjustment to take into account variations in foreign markets and currency fluctuations.

PROMOTION

Promotion can be defined as a mix of advertising, personal selling, sales promotion and public relations. The objective is to move the target customer from a position of unawareness at one end of the scale to a position of being willing to constantly buy the product at the other extreme. The customer needs to be moved through several stages from unawareness, to awareness, to knowledge, to belief in the product, to intention to buy, to continual actual purchase. It is important that no promotional activity is undertaken unless the offer and the target market have been clearly identified because it is difficult to undo promotional mistakes. Rather than rush in, it is usually better to test market to a small group before a full roll-out. Response can be measured by a variety of methods such as market surveys, focus groups (the politicians' favourite), reply coupons (with a prize draw to encourage replies) or telephone polling. It is important to know how the offer appeals to customers and if it is not working, is it because the promotional activity is ineffective or the *Product* does not appeal?

There are many promotional methods that can be used:

Personal
Face-to-face meetings with the potential customer.

The internet or perhaps intranet
Although large organizations spend millions of pounds on their websites, at the other end of the scale the internet, or internally an intranet, can be a very cheap way of promoting a product. For small organizations it has another big advantage because a well produced website is a great leveller, as customers cannot obviously tell if the website is originating from a skyscraper head office or a single desk in a back bedroom.

Direct mail
A superb mechanism for measuring the effectiveness and cost of promotional activity, especially testing. For instance, an organization thinking of sending a promotional letter with a response mechanism to a large potential customer base can firstly send a trial of ten slightly different versions to a thousand customers – a hundred of each version. Obviously the version that pulls the largest number is the one to be used.

Unfortunately as the volume of direct mail has increased over the years familiarity has reduced the response rate. Organizations using direct mail, as a primary selling tool, must now budget their operations based on a response rate as low as one per cent.

Advertising
Covers a huge gamut of everything from classified advertising to poster advertising to national TV. It has problems by way of both expense for the cost of the space and the difficulties experienced in measuring the results of advertising.

Trade exhibitions
Very hard for exhibitors to tell if they are obtaining value for money. Exhibitors are often heard to say that they only attend out of fear that they will lose out because all their competitors are there and a vague notion that customers may notice their absence.

Promotional literature
Brochures, leaflets, newsletters, posters and so on.

Press releases
A great way of obtaining free publicity in a wide variety of media – everything from a house magazine to a national newspaper. A checklist for an effective press release is:

- write an explanatory covering letter to the editor;
- supply details of launch schedule;
- list the product features (the UPBs);
- supply corporate background information;
- supply product evaluation information ideally by independent testers;
- complete technical specs are required;
- send reprints of previous related press releases or articles;
- list some current satisfied customers with contact details (user testimonials);
- supply relevant good quality pictures.

It is also important to clearly feature the product name, organization name, contact name, address, phone number, fax number and email. Make it easy for a busy editor to understand the text and be able to make personal contact. To increase the chances of being featured, press releases should be individually tailored for each publication and become even more attractive if a human interest story about the *Product* is included, or they can be linked to a current newsworthy event.

Chapter summary

- Purchasing will not prosper if it is isolated.

- Marketing comes before sales.

- Understanding the customers' needs and wants is essential.

- Consider and address the 5 Ps.

- You need to offer a unique perceived benefit.

CHAPTER 7

PRESENTATION AND SELLING SKILLS

PRESENTATIONS

The ability to make effective presentations is not strictly a part of the technical skill kit that buyers normally employ but it is now becoming ever more important as ambitious buyers wish to make their voices heard. They are realizing that the talent to stand before an audience and hold their interest and attention is both a vital business and social skill that builds confidence and demonstrates ability and professionalism. Conversely it is not a task to be undertaken by the faint hearted because an ineffective amateurish presentation will be very damaging and hard to recover from.

Very few people indeed relish the idea of standing before a group of people armed with nothing more than their voice and vocabulary. Human beings faced with a crowd of people that may be hostile are physiologically programmed to either fight or flee. To the uninitiated therefore it is a truly frightening proposition to just stand and talk, but it is reassuring to learn that nobody but nobody is a natural public speaker. It is said that even the great orator Winston Churchill was physically sick with nerves before taking to the platform to make his first public political speech. Above all, the secret to the success that anyone can obtain is hard work by way of planning, preparation, knowledge of the subject and plenty of rehearsal. Very, very few people can make a good presentation 'off the cuff'; no matter how many presentations a person makes there is no avoiding the hard work of preparation and practice.

Practice is the key so management should encourage buyers to make presentations at every conceivable opportunity.

Preparation

- Focus very carefully on the purpose and objectives of the presentation.
- Think about the audience, their aims and expectations. Put yourself in their place to decide on the best presentational style to achieve success. For instance, will a formal or informal presentation be best, backed up perhaps with PowerPoint and with or without active audience participation?
- It may be tempting to take the easy way out by taking an over informal approach. However, it is very difficult to stay in control of the meeting by just sitting around the table with the audience. Much better to stand at the front to demonstrate leadership and control of the agenda.
- Presentations can inspire, entertain, persuade, demonstrate and prove. Decide what to concentrate on.
- Essentially the basis of all good presentations is:

    1. 'Tell 'em what you are going to tell 'em.'
    2. 'Tell 'em.'
    3. 'Tell 'em again what you have just told 'em.'

    So always shape the presentation around these three sacrosanct segments.
- A thirty-minute presentation is an ambitious initial target and in a selling context is usually sufficient time to cover most circumstances. Start by breaking the subject matter into three main sections and each main section into three sub-sections. This will enable a correct timing and flow schedule to be planned that can be monitored during the course of the talk.
- It is essential that a great deal of time and effort be expended on devising very strong introduction and closing statements. The opening should be an outline of what the talk is about (tell 'em what you are going to tell 'em) and the close should be a persuasive summary of all the main elements of the talk that the audience should ideally remember (tell 'em again).
- Elicit help and constructive criticism from colleagues. It is especially important that the presentation appears professional and appropriately slick. The assistance of artistic or computer literate colleagues can be invaluable.
- Make sure the presentation follows and reinforces the brand image.
- Plan to take pressure off yourself by not talking all the time. Audience participation is always popular and can make the points you wish to

make more memorable. Remember also that the use of visual aids and illustrations can increase retention of the spoken word by up to 70 per cent. On the subject of factual retention it has been calculated that information that is Read people retain 10 per cent of subject matter, Heard 20 per cent, Seen 30 per cent, Heard and Seen 50 per cent, Said 70 per cent, Said & Done 90 per cent. Remember also that the concentration span of the average listener is only six to eight minutes at a time.

- Produce a handout, notes or a copy of the presentation for your audience to take away – providing it is relevant and useful to them, not something that will be thrown into the nearest available waste paper bin. Ensure handouts and notes follow and reinforce the branding.
- Good relevant quotations are a useful way of adding gravitas and interest to the talk. Always credit the source of the quotation even if it is 'Anon'.
- Examples, statistics and experiences can also hold the audience's attention.
- Unless you are very good at telling jokes and always get a laugh, avoid them like the plague.
- Plan and control the room, such as seating positions, in which the presentation takes place. Make sure that any technology works and you know how to use it. Always have some sort of alternative back-up available. Take nothing for granted, check and double check everything.

Practice, rehearsal and delivery of the presentation

- Devise your own prompts, perhaps cue cards, but beware nerves can lead to the dropping or muddling of cards. Better to have the headings and sub-headings on one piece of A4 paper with prompts for the whole presentation written very clearly in five columns. The first column to cover the prompts for the opening statement, the next three columns for the main section and the fifth column for the close. Make sure the prompts are listed clearly enough to be seen at a quick glance.
- The presentation should be in your own words and appear to be fairly spontaneous. Never read from a written script because it will come across as mind-numbingly boring to the audience.
- Rehearse the talk into a tape recorder and play it back to yourself and colleagues to hone and refine it. Once you are satisfied play it back to yourself again and again in order to make its contents second nature. A

long drive can be an ideal opportunity to hammer home the content by undisturbed listening to the tape several times.

- Better still is to use a video camera in a similar way – but not in the car!
- When you practise in the actual room you will invariably find that your delivery is not loud enough. A colleague will help get the volume right – probably when the level is right you will think that you are shouting. Help is also required to make sure that you do not speak too quickly, again only you will think that your speaking unnaturally slowly when it is right.
- The style and language used should reflect the expectations of the audience. For instance, a presentation to a legal department would probably be more formal in content and language than, say, to a creative audience.
- Be aware of body language and mannerisms (See Chapter 11, page 109). Once again helpful colleagues will have pointed out your annoying habits at the rehearsal stage.
- Come the day try to relax and before you start take some deep breaths from the pit of the stomach to slow down your metabolic rate and always smile, smile, smile. Do not be afraid to let your personality and natural enthusiasm shine through.
- Know your carefully devised opening statement off by heart so that you could even quote it verbatim in your sleep. This way nerves will not interrupt your opening flow and a solid opening will build confidence and demonstrate that the audience is supportive and on your side. It is vital that this opening is right because the first four to seven seconds is the time zone that establishes audience mood and rapport.
- Everyone is scared at this point but a certain amount of adrenaline is essential to the performance, just ignoring the nerves and focusing on getting on with it is the key to success. In the words of Frederich Nietzsche 'What doesn't kill makes you stronger'.
- Make eye contact continuously with all the audience and keep looking happy.
- After a couple of minutes ask the audience at the back if they can hear you well.
- Pauses now and again are to be encouraged; once again only you will feel that they are lasting five minutes when in actual fact they are only a few seconds. The audience will not even notice.

- If rude people start to talk amongst themselves just stop and look at them. They will stop immediately, be embarrassed and your authority will soar with the rest of the audience.
- Don't worry if you don't know the answer to a question. Rather than flannel admit that you do not have the answer currently to hand but that you will get back to them with an answer within a specified time. You may be comfortable taking questions as you go along; if not, say in your opening statement that you will take them at the end (before the closing statement).
- Most of the points listed here for making a presentation to a group apply equally well, though perhaps in not so much depth, when making a presentation to an individual.
- Almost as important as the opening statement is the close. It is best to finish with a flourish on a high and positive note ideally with the audience wanting more. This is the point when you will finally relax and start enjoying the ordeal!

SALES TECHNIQUES

Most sales people who have received sales training will be familiar with a programme known as 'The seven steps to making a sale'. It is worth bearing in mind that this is a basic, fairly unsophisticated approach to the art of selling but most buyers will at least recognize from experience some of the techniques listed that have been employed on them many times. The seven steps are:

1. Planning and preparation
2. Introduction and opening
3. Questioning
4. Presentation
5. Overcoming objections
6. Closing the sale
7. After sales responsibilities.

Step one – planning and preparation

- Generally this includes a great deal of research of both the marketplace and the client requirements and the way they operate. Remember marketing always comes before sales.

- It is essential that the sales contact knows their own product or service inside out. There is no substitute for product knowledge.
- It is also essential to know the existing supply arrangements and make an assessment of the reaction of the existing supplier if their position is threatened. Some initial contingency planning is therefore required. Can and will they match your offer? What are the strengths and weaknesses of the competition?
- Identify the key decision makers and influencers. Assess what makes them tick both objectively (business requirements) and subjectively (emotional and personal feelings).
- Identify the internal politics that may influence the decision-making process.
- Identify business parameters that may influence, for instance, length of existing contracts, budgets, year-end implications and so on.
- The strategic implications, issues, priorities and problems.
- Prepare a list of relevant questions that may be new or reinforce what is already known from the market research already conducted.
- Focus on the objectives for the meeting and plan and organize to achieve this.

Step two – introduction and opening

- Begin with a firm confident handshake, smile, look them in the eye, behave professionally and take comfort from the fact that you are well prepared and know your subject.
- Never be late for a meeting.
- Introduce yourself and what your business is about.
- Find out how much time the customer has for the meeting and politely ask if it is OK to take notes as you wish to thoroughly understand their requirements.
- Set the scene, establish rapport and put your customer at ease by talking about common ground and asking general questions that are easy to answer. Sales people often keep a 'little black book' of their client's personal details – hobbies, family, sports interests and so on.

Step three – questioning

- Move to step three when the time is right to outline the proposal and begin to ask more nitty gritty questions.

- The right questions are vital to identify the key items in the offer that will provide recognizable advantages to the customer. They will also flush out possible problems and identify ways of solving them.
- Questioning is also a way of bringing rapport and trust to a burgeoning relationship. This is because most people would rather talk than listen and appreciate somebody who takes the time and trouble to enquire about their work and how it affects them personally.
- During the questioning stage the customer should be doing more than 80 per cent of the talking; if not, either the questions are wrong or there may be a personality or political clash that is clouding the issue. If the clash is irrevocable it may be better to withdraw gracefully at this stage to discuss alternatives with colleagues and live to fight another day.
- At this point ask open questions – ones that cannot be answered with a straight yes or no. For instance questions that begin with who, what, why, where, when or how.
- 'Why?' is a very good word to explore an initial answer in more depth.
- 'Can you tell me more about how?' works well as an opening question especially with senior contacts that have a good grasp of the wider picture.
- Once asked it is best to be quiet and listen, do not interrupt, always let your customer reply fully to their complete satisfaction. Maintain good eye contact and show that you understand both their answers and their feelings – especially important when you are probing their personal motives and emotions.
- Do not proceed until you are sure that you understand the answers that are offered. Do not begin to offer solutions until the questioning has been completed because it is essential that you consider and reflect on the total picture. Do not make snap judgements based only on partial information.
- It pays to summarize your assessment and understanding of the situation at the end of the open question session. If some of the answers have been vague it is useful to clarify the situation by asking some closed questions – ones that are phrased in such a manner that they will only produce a yes or no reply. For example, 'Can you confirm that all the electronic contracts we discussed expire at the end of March?'
- The astute questioner will all the time have been probing to discover the strategic impact and implications that the offer may imply to the customer together with the softer issues by way of political and personal feeling barriers that will need to be overcome.

Step four – presentation

- The techniques for making successful presentations to groups are discussed extensively at the beginning of this chapter. Presentations to individuals follow many of the same principles but are usually shorter and more informal.
- Never lose sight or distort the central proposition especially if it has already been agreed at senior level. However, the sales presentation must address the individual person's needs, priorities, constraints and motives that are particular to them. The message will therefore need tweaking to emphasize the pertinent advantages. Singing from the same hymn sheet is therefore essential when several members of staff are involved in the sales process.
- At all times it is important to keep control of the presentation but in a friendly and relaxed way. Don't waffle if you don't know the answer to a question, admit it and just specify when you will go back with the answer.

Step five – overcoming objections

- Great play is made in sales manuals of the importance of mastering the skill of overcoming objections. However, if the marketing has been successful by way of the right unique perceived benefit (UPB) for the client and the presentation has addressed any concerns, there need not necessarily be any major objections. However, in the real world there are always some awkward folk who will insist on having their say and there are a few golden rules to adhere to.
- Objections, however apparently irrelevant or trivial, should be addressed constructively starting perhaps by a question such as 'why do you say that?' This is a good way to flush out misgivings and misunderstandings.
- It may be necessary to probe deeper to discover the real issues. The best way to cope with an emotional subjective reaction is to gently switch the discussion back into talking about relevant facts.
- Do not get into an argument. Even if you win, it is only winning a battle, as you are certain to lose the war.
- Do not use the word 'but', it is invariably subconsciously taken to be confrontational.
- If the objections have been overcome successfully and honestly you will detect a certain warmth beginning to creep into the meeting.

Step six – closing the sale

- Providing the previous five steps have been successful, especially in an internal sales situation, closing the sale should merely be a summary of the agreement that has been reached.
- However, there is an enormous amount of sales folklore around covering the various tricks that can be used to close a sale. Just for the record and for the amusement of buyers some of the more popular traditional attempts to close are:
  - *The signature close* – 'Do you want to use my pen to sign the order?'
  - *The alternative close* – 'Shall we deliver next Monday or Wednesday?'
  - *The challenge close* – 'You will probably need to refer to your boss for a decision?'
  - *The ego close* – 'We find that only our most discerning clients buy this level of quality and service.'
  - *The negative close* – 'I'm sorry but due to factory holidays we cannot deliver in less than three weeks.'
  - *The guilt close* – 'It may appear to be a large initial pay-out but you do need to protect yourself with the security our product offers.'
  - *The sympathy close* – 'I have had a bad time lately and my boss is really on my back to secure this order.'
  - *The cuddly toy close* – 'Let me leave it with you to try out, we will not invoice until next month.'
  - *The pros and cons list* – 'Just let us take a few minutes to list the benefits and disadvantages to help you reach a decision.'
  - *The last ditch close*, on the way out – 'It must be me because I know this product is right for you so please tell me where I have gone wrong.'

Step seven – after sales responsibilities

- The agreement should also cover key performance indicators (KPIs) schedules, policies and procedures. All should be carefully documented and signed off by both parties.
- Customers will quite rightly hold the sales person responsible for first class subsequent performance, therefore excellent follow-up communication must be maintained especially by way of regular progress and problem reporting.
- Continuous improvement must constantly remain the name of the game!

SALES INTERVIEW MONITORING

This chapter has listed a great number of points to be considered to make a successful sales proposal. It may therefore be helpful, especially for the inexperienced, to offer some advice on the major areas to focus on and thus be able to judge how the interview is going. If you tackle and succeed in the following areas you will be successful.

- **Seeing the other person's point of view**. By putting yourself in their shoes you will gain an appreciation what angle they are coming from – even if you do not agree. Forearmed is forewarned to signpost the way you can best lead the discussion.
- **Building rapport**. Aim to obtain agreement on a summary of the current situation in factual non-controversial terms and encourage them to state any problems or worries they have. Do not express or even imply any criticism, as you do not want to elicit any defensive responses. This is the time for building bridges and hopefully a budding friendship.
- **Quantifying problems**. If you have done your homework you will be able to quote a few facts and figures that illustrate that it would be in their own interest for them to seek out new ways to solve the problem.
- **Offer a solution**. Be sympathetic saying you understand how difficult life can be but this is one problem you can take off their hands. Make them an offer they can't refuse by coming up with a clearly considered solution.

Chapter summary

- Presentational skills are becoming more important for buyers.

- Preparation and practice is the key to success.

- Buyers do not necessarily know much about selling.

- A knowledge of sales techniques will help buyers to both communicate better internally and counteract the hard sell from outside.

CHAPTER 8

THE PRACTICAL APPLICATION OF MARKETING AND SALES THEORY

THE CUSTOMER IS KING

For a purchasing department the switch to a marketing, customer-focused operation is not a step to be taken lightly because it usually involves major cultural and behavioural changes for the entire team. Buyers instinctively concentrate on looking to the outside world, not only because it is an important part of their work, but also because it is easier to relate to suppliers as they are likely to be less challenging than internal colleagues. Indeed some buyers seem to glorify in the praise and adulation that sales people often shower upon them. There is a need for the buying team to acknowledge that the customer is king and that their very existence in the organization depends to a large extent on customer satisfaction. It must not be, as office gossip will frequently suggest, always a 'them and us' situation with internal customers. To counteract this negative attitude a team effort needs to be encouraged in order to pursue a policy of persuading internal customers of the merits of jointly working together to contribute improvements to both the bottom line and competitive advantage. A few carefully planned team away days will be required to clarify a new mission statement, the strategy, alterations to systems, policies and procedures and perhaps even draw up changes to methods of working and job descriptions.

MARKET RESEARCH

Theory dictates that the crux of marketing is to find out your customers' real needs and desires and then to create and promote a product or service that fulfils that need and desire. This is a difficult issue, but one that must be thoroughly dealt with, not only because it is hard to obtain in-depth reliable information, but it may also throw up awkward and unpleasant issues such as the potential customer thinks that the buying department is a waste of space!

Take heart, however, you will not be alone as a 2004 survey (reported in *Supply Management* magazine, 16 December 2004) of just one procurement category by spend management solutions company Ariba revealed that 60 per cent of the purchasers interviewed admitted that marketing staff were suspicious of procurement professionals. In addition more than half of purchasing managers revealed that they had little involvement in the spending of marketing budgets.

How then to find out the customers' real needs and desires? There is no alternative but to take a leaf out of the marketers' book and undertake some basic market research using customer survey questionnaires. Delving deep for answers to a whole series of questions concerning their real requirements and also most importantly their opinions of the services they think are available to them currently and what they think they would really like. Answers need to be straight from the hip with no punches pulled. The questionnaire should also incorporate a 'health check' of the customer's current operations for two reasons: firstly to gain information about their strengths and weaknesses and secondly people usually like to talk about their work and it will help break the ice. Careful consideration therefore needs to be given to the questions that should be asked. However, market research is not a one-off operation; initially the research will be about gathering facts about the potential customers' current spend by interrogating the finance department's ledgers. As has been stated many times in this book the amount of *spend, by whom, on what, with whom* really does need to be analysed and understood in detail. Only when this has been accomplished satisfactorily should any attempt be made to even begin to question the customer and this will need to be done across a range of staff. Subsequently, as part of a continuous improvement programme, research will always be needed to monitor the customers' changing requirements.

Often it is too simplistic to think that there is just one decision maker who needs convincing. In their book *Organisational Buying Behaviour* (1992) Frederick Webster and Yoram Wind identified the people who are involved in buying decisions as the Decision-Making Unit (DMU) and listed them in five roles:

- users of the product or service;
- providers of technical expertise who influence the buying decision;
- selectors of the supplier or product or both;
- controllers of information flow;
- negotiation participants and order placers.

Frequently DMUs do not work together in any formal sense, but it is well to carefully consider all concerned, as an influencer can just as easily scupper a decision as a user.

Various collection methods can be employed for the principal market research survey that will consist of both an assessment of the strengths and weaknesses of the customers' current buying operation plus an investigation to find out their real needs and wants. This will need to be done across a range of staff at all levels to obtain the true picture. Purchasing staff can ask the customers themselves or perhaps send out an email survey form – both pretty unproductive techniques, as it is probable that unbiased honest opinions would not be obtained by these methods. Worse still in the case of emails, as frequently they can be deleted or ignored. The best way to obtain buy-in is when the survey is part of a review of the entire organization's procurement that has received the wholehearted backing of the CEO and the Board of Directors, or at the very least a senior powerful champion. If there is a possibility of resistance and conflict it would be better to ask a neutral manager from another department, maybe accounts, internal audit or secretariat to actually ask the face-to-face questions. An effective, though expensive, approach is to use an outside consultant who is experienced in asking probing questions. The customer will also be more likely to open up in confidence, as they will more readily identify with an outsider who has 'no axes to grind'. Best of all will be to use a specialist market research organization but this is likely to be very expensive unless your marketing department can do a special deal. Failing that, maybe there is someone in the marketing department studying for their professional qualifications who would help as part of a research project or case study.

It will definitely be a good idea to test market the questionnaire on existing established customers to assess the reactions before launching it on possibly difficult or resistant new customers. It can then be improved in stages. It is difficult for any researcher to march into a maverick buying area and start asking questions without being expected and without authority, so it is important that any initiative does receive the backing of senior management to open the door. A basic draft format for the questionnaire is included in Chapter 9, page 95.

Another important source of opinion to survey is suppliers. They can be asked how well your own professional buyers rate in comparison to their other customers. Sometimes this comparison can also be made with a common supplier against the potential customer's procurement skills. Suppliers are in a good position to be able to judge against other purchasers, maybe even your competitors. Once again probing questions need to be addressed to suppliers coupled with an emphasis that honest uncensored answers are required – 'warts and all', coupled with an assurance that there will definitely be no adverse comeback to threaten the relationship.

A properly conducted survey revealing hearts and minds answers from both internal customers and suppliers will probably produce unexpected, even unpleasant, shocks. However, it will provide telling evidence to show the whole purchasing team the areas where improvements are required to their own performance as well as reinforce some of their opinions of customers' foibles. It should therefore produce an impetus to making sure your own house is in order before attempting any expansion initiative.

PRODUCING A MARKETING AND SALES PLAN

Armed with the information obtained from an in-depth survey of the customers' actual procurement needs and wants, a marketing and sales plan can be produced. It should consist of the following steps:

- analysis (Where are we now – our strengths and weaknesses? What do our current and potential customers expect, want and need?);
- planning (Where do we want to be and how do we get there?);
- implementation (marketing and selling in action);
- monitoring (measuring and continuously improving our performance).

Initially not all of the marketing and sales plan needs to be set in tablets of stone, as it may be desirable to segment the target market and deal with it in stages, giving the flexibility to cope in varying ways with the individual idiosyncrasies of internal customers. This approach can also be an educational advantage, as a steep learning curve will be experienced and segmentation will enable continuous improvement and fine-tuning to be employed.

ANALYSIS

Assuming initial market research has produced reliable information, because it has been double-checked, its analysis will usually throw up that there are some traumatic decisions and radical changes to be made. Seldom will it reveal that everything in the garden is lovely – even with established internal customers. Indeed if it were all favourable there would be no maverick buying going on anywhere and purchasing would already be a major decision maker amongst the board room hierarchy. In most organizations to become truly customer focused will take a radical change to the purchasing culture as well as dictating a great deal of business re-engineering of working practices and procedures.

One of the difficult areas to judge objectively is the emotive issue of heavy critical comment, especially when it appears to be purely subjective. It is suggested that a measured pause by stepping back should be adopted to avoid an emotional reaction in the same vein. After all, purchasing people are good at making objective judgements and are usually fairly thick-skinned. If in doubt seek the opinion of trusted neutrals to assess if the bad comments should be taken into account, or discarded because they are merely malicious and not constructive.

It is suggested that the research results be used in the same manner that an outside consultancy would do to ensure that every area of the purchasing operation throughout the organization is taken into account. A good starting point is to compare the total spend of the organization with the current spend that is controlled by Purchasing. The trick is then to operate as a business within a business; the total organizational spend being taken as the market potential and thus the target for Purchasing is to achieve an ever increasing market share, with the eventual goal of becoming the monopoly supplier.

Marketing decisions have also to be made, once again using the research and especially the expectation gap model (Figure 6.1 page 62), to finalize the *Offer* – a clearly defined *Product* that is in a strong *Position* to attract and win over the target customers. Making a start by producing lists of plus and minus points of the current *Offer* will quickly identify areas of concern to be addressed. However, there should also be a very positive list of plus points, especially if the performance measures advocated earlier in this book have been adopted. The professional approach and skill set of a well trained and motivated buying team should be an attraction to any potential customer, especially when the expectation gap has been bridged.

A SWOT analysis (strengths, weaknesses, opportunities and threats) involving the whole purchasing team in a brainstorming session will also produce excellent results and help to reinforce the validity of the plus and minus lists. Typically the team will identify *Strengths* such as:

- a professional approach
- full-time buying roles offering more commitment
- trained specialists with professional qualifications, for example, CIPS (Chartered Institute of Purchasing & Supply)
- commercial acumen
- experienced negotiators
- ability to obtain better value for money
- marketplace knowledge
- objective measurement techniques employed
- contract expertise
- ethically sound
- nice people to do business with!

Weaknesses will be obtained from analysing the market research. Some replies will be valid and supply ample food for thought, others will be based on a lack of knowledge of the skill and expertise that purchasing professionals offer. This lack of knowledge by the customer reinforces the need for marketing and selling the function properly.

Opportunities include the potential for increasing market share and curbing maverick buying that will bring benefits to the purchasing department and even more importantly to the organization as a whole, in terms of bottom line and competitive advantage.

Threats. The outsourcing of purchasing is becoming more fashionable and departments that stand still and do not raise their profile within the organization place themselves at greater risk. Another fashion is decentralization and if this is not managed well it can lead to a wholesale increase in maverick buying resulting in fewer jobs for buyers.

PLANNING TIPS

Obviously planning in detail cannot begin until the objectives (to become the monopoly supplier) and strategy (to be a wholly customer-focused operation) have been finalized and accepted by the entire team. A carefully considered customer care programme will help greatly in this respect.

Before Abbey National floated on the stock exchange in the late eighties it was felt that a key factor in being successful in a more competitive environment was to improve service to the customer. In order to change the culture across the entire organization of around 25 000 employees, a two-day customer care programme was initially devised which every Abbey National staff member had to attend – from the Chairman down to the newest recruit in the post room. About thirty people, selected at random, attended each session. Attendees were mixed up so the Chairman may well have attended the same session as the latest post room recruit. The cost was enormous but paid off massively as both market share and share price steadily increased during the early nineties. Unfortunately a change of top management resulted in the customer care programme being discontinued and this was probably one factor in the subsequent decline of the company, leading to a take over by the Spanish bank, Banco Santander in 2004.

Early consideration should also be given to producing a strong *brand* image. Invariably a mere mention of the words 'brand image or branding' will produce a verbal barrage of cynicism. But large corporations do not spend millions of pounds on brand creation, design and promotion for no reason. Consider, for instance, the money that was spent on re-branding of BP with a new circular green and yellow logo or the innovative genius that launched the original hugely successful marketing campaign for the Orange mobile phone name and branding. To get it wrong can also be disastrous – witness the embarrassment and cost for British Airways when they had to drop the idea of placing modern art on the tail fins of their aeroplanes. An original brand image can successfully reinforce differentiation and promote feelings of trust, reliability and professionalism in the minds of the customer. It is also fun to involve the entire team in the creation of a logo and slogan/strap line. The logo needs to be a creative and original design combined with a meaningful and memorable slogan that communicates expertise, reliability and help to the customer. Maybe something like 'Supply solutions' or 'Purchasing pays dividends'? Once chosen, the brand will require promoting, for instance, on all correspondence and written communications including emails. Other promotion possibilities are the house magazine, posters on notice boards and perhaps even freebies like T-shirts and drinks mats.

Careful planning of the sales campaign is essential, employing the best techniques for influencing the target customers favourably. When thinking about a sales campaign some of the items worth considering are:

- Finding out who are the decision makers amongst your target customers.
- Conducting as much prior research as possible – for instance, investigating financial accounts to establish how much the internal customer's purchasing spend, on what and with whom. Or gain the information from their suppliers and the marketplace.
- Carefully focus on the areas to concentrate on. Maybe it will be best to initially go for the less contentious, not very political, lower profile opportunities. At other times it will be opportune to instigate a major change management project that requires board approval and buy-in.
- Finding the best ways of opening doors to gain their interest and attention. What level of management backing is required?
- Using your boss or his boss to influence and network with senior management and the head of department of your target market.
- It is usually essential to find a high-level champion of the cause and make sure that they are very well briefed on the advantages of the offer.
- Judging whether formal presentations or face-to-face meetings are best.
- Embed the culture that Purchasing operates as a business within a business.
- Deciding who amongst the purchasing team are the people most likely to succeed. Some people take naturally to selling more than others who require further training.
- Producing a sales brochure either in printed format or on the intranet via departmental web pages. However, do not rely on this, as it will only be a minor influencer.
- Writing a monthly newsletter highlighting success stories. Problem – who has the time to compose it?
- Devising a special offer to gain attention.
- Impressing them with well organized supplier conferences that they are invited to attend as observers.
- Offering to supply them with a solution to a problem they are experiencing.
- Better still ask them to help you with a problem – flattery often works!
- Copying the successful sales techniques that salesmen of the suppliers selling to Purchasing employ.

- Organizing inter-departmental staff exchanges to break down barriers and 'them and us' situations by learning about each other's work and culture.
- Setting up cross-functional teams – vital for all major procurement projects.
- Promoting an organizational culture that purchasing is a proactive not a reactive activity. The message is that the earlier professional buyers are involved the greater their contribution will be.

In marketing theory *Price* is heavily featured, but it is only of concern in a marketing context for purchasing departments that charge out their services. In this case it is suggested that perhaps discounted charging can apply to new customers or better still introduce a price promise as part of the KPIs (key performance indicators), that cost savings will always exceed charges. For departments that do not charge out, price can be prominently billed as a positive free benefit for the customer. Busy managers may be won over by being offered an extra resource at no cost.

Target markets have been mentioned previously and it makes sense to prioritize in order not to overstretch resources and to set realistic time scales. Remember it is fatal to make promises in the *Offer* and subsequently not deliver.

Don't forget measurements of success and objectives set both for individuals and the department. Of course the principal sales and marketing objective to be measured is the increase in market share.

IMPLEMENTATION

At the same time as the marketing planning, another major factor to consider is how best to target and roll out the selling effort. Perhaps for a maverick buyer spending a low budget as a relatively small peripheral part of their working activity it may be best for a peer group buyer from the Purchasing Department to sell to them the benefits of leaving it to the professionals. Or perhaps the Purchasing Manager can yield sufficient power and authority to persuade members of his management peer group of the error of their and their staff's ways. However, when aiming for the large-spend, potential new customer areas it is better to start from the top, treating each area as a market sector that requires a business-to-business major account selling approach.

Follow the examples of large corporations such as Xerox, IBM and the international consultancies who open the door of a sales campaign at the very top in the boardroom before it cascades down to other members of their sales team who promote and implement the top-level decision throughout the organization.

Modern business-to-business selling aims to produce UPB's (unique perceived benefits) in the way of tailored products and services that deliver major strategic benefits to the business. It implies that the concept must be sold to customer contacts that have a sound grasp of the total business strategy. This invariably dictates that the first people that will need to be convinced are at senior, probably boardroom level. It also pays to have a champion at this level – the financial director is ideal, as he or she will readily grasp the financial implication of the advantages of adopting co-ordinated strategic purchasing throughout the organization. Selling at a high strategic level has a huge advantage because it leaves the competition that continues to target middle managers and buyers way behind. At the lower level their contacts do not have the visionary authority to make radical change and they will not even have the inclination to try if they perceive a personal threat. It is also very difficult to raise the contact level later if the initial approach is too low down the pecking order because control is reduced when the reliance on escalating the proposal has been partially relinquished.

Typically the adoption of a business-to-business major account scenario would require the following stages of work to be carried out:

1.   Make use of the work already undertaken by way of measuring, marketing and sales planning to approach a senior or director level strategic decision maker and convince them of the benefits of measuring purchasing performance and the adoption of a strategic approach to the management of the supply chain. The key message is pointing out that the organization is losing out because professional purchasing is only being carried out on a portion of the total spend. Figures should be presented to show the additional contribution to bottom line profit that could be obtained if all the procurement was rationalized to take advantage of such items as economies of scale and increased commercial acumen. Present the figures in balance sheet profit and loss terms because this is what directors are comfortable with analysing and discussing. The objective may be to have the new champion influence and persuade members of his

or her peer group who undertake their own buying of the need for change or to open the door to making a comprehensive presentation to the full Board to review the organization's entire procurement operation.

2.   If the presentation to the Board route is undertaken the choice of presenter is crucial. The person must be comfortable in boardroom surroundings, know the subject inside out and display sufficient authority for board members to take the proposal very seriously. It goes without saying that the presentation must be professional, impressive and extremely persuasive. The bigger the prospect, either by way of spend or organizational political clout, the more planning and preparation will be required.

The objectives are to sell the advantages of the UPB – generally it is best to concentrate on one very strong strategic organizational benefit. In this case it will be along the lines of 'that by adopting professional strategic purchasing throughout the organization profits will be increased substantially'. For a not-for-profit organization the focus could be on massive cost savings and better value for money. Generally people respond best to a single point of interest especially if it is perceived as an innovative and very strong strategic benefit to the whole organization. A case study could be an example of what the Purchasing Department has already achieved. A Board decision will be requested on the way forward to achieve the benefits. Two scenarios may be suggested, one way is to bring in outside consultants or the other preferred route (that can be sold as cheaper and better) is to employ the Purchasing Department to manage a broad-ranging review because they already have the experience. An agreement to a timetable for the production of a Board Report will also be required. Inevitably there will be difficult questions. In organizations that have 'Robber Baron' directors working in silos some of the questions will be highly political. The presenter should best duck these and just concentrate on giving 'sweetness and light' factual answers. Handled correctly by focusing on the USB no one can reasonably object to a review of procurement when such a huge potential prize is being dangled.

3.   A successful Board presentation will have produced buy-in and support from the top – which always goes a long way. The review also provides the perfect entrée into all the target non-conforming

areas to analyse and question exactly what is going on – perfect for obtaining sound market research information.

4.   The review will inevitably highlight areas where drastic changes will be required and some may be very unpalatable to directors, managers and staff. To only propose changes in a report to the Board will be asking for trouble because of the animosity that it will arouse. Much better to negotiate and agree changes with decision makers before publication, not forgetting that Purchasing are in a strong position because they are merely carrying out the wishes of the Board. The Board report can then highlight the changes that have been agreed – giving of course munificent credit to the participating new customer department heads. It will also reiterate the targets and highlight the timetable for producing results.

5.   Make sure that the agreed changes are signed off by all concerned.

6.   Report progress to the Board at least once a quarter. Remember that it is best to agree major changes with department heads but this will not always be possible – sometimes the approval of the Board will be required to generate action.

In order for changes to be implemented satisfactorily, Purchasing staff will need to be very clear about the features and benefits of the UPB offer – everybody should be 'singing from the same hymn sheet' when the sales and promotion programme swings into action. Sales is the 'make things happen' stage that acts as the follow-up to the marketing initiative. Any successful sales campaign requires careful planning and needs to be undertaken at all levels of the new customer's operation. However, it is a skill which needs to be learnt. Training will inevitably be required, whilst they may think that they know all about selling without concentrated training they will certainly fall flat on their face. Persuading the Sales Director to allocate some spaces on training programmes to buyers is economical and often works out very well because of the interaction between colleagues from different disciplines. Sales training is beneficial in two ways because it is an additional skill for buyers that will help them in their day-to-day buying negotiation as well as teaching them to sell internally. There is a strong argument for advocating that one out of every three training courses that buyers attend should have a selling element.

Distribution often needs to be considered because it may be necessary for instance to relocate buyers to sit in the customer's department to overcome objections, learn about the products and gain the confidence of staff. Computer systems may also require integration improvements.

MONITORING

KPIs, policies and procedures will need to be agreed, documented and signed off. Subsequent performance must be carefully monitored and fed back by regular face-to-face meetings with the customer to embed confidence. As an additional spin off these regular meetings can also be an opportunity to learn about future sales opportunities. Management will need to be sensitive to any fine-tuning requirements as matters proceed and have contingency arrangements in place in the event of problems. Demonstrable continuous improvement must always be the name of the game.

Chapter summary

- Good market research is vital.

- Obtaining reliable needs and wants information is difficult but essential.

- Target the real decision makers and influencers.

- Involve everyone in drawing up a marketing and sales plan.

- Decide at what level to target your effort – segmentation or a take-over?

- Buyers are not natural sales people – they will require training.

- Convince a top-level Champion.

CHAPTER 9

MARKETING RESEARCH QUESTIONNAIRE – SAMPLE QUESTIONS

SETTING THE SCENE

As a result of being impressed with the Purchasing Department having put into practice the performance measurement and reporting measures listed earlier in this book, your neutral researchers will hopefully carry the backing of the Board, or at least a senior influential champion. They will then have the credibility and authority to approach potential new customer buying areas stating that they are part of a team that has been charged with finding out how buying is conducted throughout the organization.

The researchers will need the skill and sensitivity to be able to select the right questions and change the emphasis according to who is being interviewed. For instance, a departmental manger will be asked more strategic and less detailed questions than the person who is dealing with the day-to-day buying activity. To put people at their ease it is best that the opening questions are of a general nature about the department and the work as people usually like talking about their work. A relaxed open conversational environment should be encouraged, a good idea is for researchers to make it a two-way street by soliciting and being very open to questions from the interviewee. It is very important to emphasize during the opening discussion that if any personal opinions are expressed during the course of the interview they will remain strictly confidential.

Some people will have some reservations and may express their reticence by being awkward about arranging an interview. Confrontation is certainly not desirable at this point so it will take diplomacy and persuasion backed by a touch of firmness to overcome any stonewalling. For instance it may be beneficial to gently point out that a deadline for presenting a report to senior management must be adhered to. Subsequently always arrive on time for an interview.

This questionnaire format is designed to cover a wider gamut of possible questions than may be required, from asking a buying assistant to the departmental head, leaving the researcher to pick and mix as appropriate.

The interviewer should as part of the interview always ask for copies or borrow any relevant documentation that are mentioned in discussion, such as procedure manuals, as they will be useful in the preparation of a later report.

As part of the planning process for the interview a copy of the interviewee's job description should be obtained from the human resources department to familiarize the interviewer with the organization's interpretation of the job requirements.

During the interview remember the power of wording the questions to make them open or closed to suit the circumstances as the session goes along (See Chapter 8, page 76).

OPENING QUESTIONS

As mentioned previously, the researcher should use the opening session to create a laid-back, non-confrontational atmosphere. At first therefore it is better to talk in general terms about the research project or their job and only ask questions that are easy to answer and in no way can be perceived as a veiled threat. However, if after a while it becomes obvious that the interviewee is determined to be unco-operative and hostile, despite all efforts of rapprochement, it may be necessary to suggest foreclosing the discussion calmly stating disappointment at the lack of progress. Often this will bring a change in the interviewee's demeanour as they begin to ponder the consequences and the interview can usually be successfully resurrected.

Remember always steer clear of arguments no matter how much provocation is shown.

1.   Ask them to give an outline of their job and the department, paying particular regard to the procurement aspects. *Hopefully this will break the ice, especially if the interviewer does not know the*

interviewee. Show great interest, prompt them and ask questions about their work, such as job satisfaction, if there is any initial reluctance.

2. Clarify if buying is a full-time occupation or just a peripheral part of the interviewee's job.

3. How much time is spent on buying? *Obviously this will be an estimate that may be worthwhile checking later with management – often the two estimates are poles apart!*

4. What commodities do they buy? *Probe to capture the full range.*

5. Do they like buying? *Good general question to diffuse any uncomfortable atmosphere.*

6. What do they dislike about buying? *Ditto general question.*

7. Roughly how many suppliers do they deal with on a regular basis?

8. How much does their department spend annually on products and services?

9. How much is their own annual spend responsibility? *Very often interviewees will not have a clue about any spend figures. Do not on any account make the interviewee uncomfortable about this obvious inefficiency, don't even raise an eyebrow!*

10. If spend figures are available ask for details of the annual spend they are accountable for by commodity ('top ten' lists are best). *If available ask for copies.*

11. Same question broken down by supplier.

12. How many purchase orders/contracts do they raise per annum?

13. Do they make the buying decision or are purchase orders they raise merely a rubber stamping of decisions made by others?

14. Are they responsible for any stock holdings? *If so, ask for details such as value of holding, stock turn per annum, administration and distribution costs and so on.*

15. Can they easily obtain up-to-date management information from the IT systems?

16. Ask to see details of the management information that is available. *Hopefully they will display on-screen information that can lead into a rundown of the entire purchasing system.*

17. How much does the buying function cost? *A question for management.*

18. Do they have any purchasing problems or have they had any bad buying experiences?

19. Ask and encourage them to relate success stories about their own purchasing experiences.

SUPPLY SIDE QUESTIONS

1. How often are supplying sources reviewed?
2. Is this a formal documented process?
3. Are they satisfied with their current supplier portfolio?
4. How do you find new suppliers?
5. How are suppliers assessed for areas such as financial strength, quality of workforce and management, volume capability, quality assurance, reliability and so on.
6. Are most suppliers local? *Probe to find out if local suppliers are preferred. It may illustrate narrow parochial attitudes.*
7. Is there an approved supplier list in operation?
8. Are there any formal procedures for adding or deleting suppliers from the approved supplier database?
9. Who makes these decisions and based on what evidence?
10. Who is responsible for expediting and progress chasing?
11. Are supplier visits both for evaluation and quality assurance purposes encouraged and made regularly?
12. How is supplier performance monitored and measured?
13. Is there a documented vendor rating system in place? *Important to understand how any system works and if it is an effective practical tool.*
14. Is a supplier development programme operated? *If yes, obtain details.*

POLICY AND PROCEDURE QUESTIONS

1. Is there a documented procedure manual? *Borrow a copy.*
2. How often is it reviewed?
3. Is there a purchasing work flowchart available?
4. Ask probing questions about the segregation of duties aspects to assess that the organization is sufficiently well protected against fraud by buyers, suppliers or by the collusion of both. For example, how effective are the delegated authorities and segregation by way of signatures on purchase orders, goods received notes (GRNs) and invoice approvals?
5. Is there a visible audit trail?
6. Must a number of competitive quotes be obtained?
7. Are they restricted to accepting the lowest tender or can value judgements be made when it is beneficial?

8. Are there circumstances when only one quote is obtained? Is this an acceptable practice?
9. If only one quote is received or the lowest quote is not accepted, how is this justified formally, for instance, to answer future audit enquires or to allay accusations of impropriety?
10. When was the area last independently audited? *Request a copy or it may have been possible to have already obtained a copy from other sources as a part of the interview planning process.*
11. Is there a written ethical code in place covering dealings with suppliers including the permitted levels of entertainment, hospitality and gifts?
12. Are records maintained of any hospitality received?
13. Does hospitality require prior approval?
14. Ask for the interviewee's own opinions on the issue of ethics. *Perhaps they are naïve, too open, self-opinionated, prejudiced or possess other traits that unscrupulous suppliers could take advantage of. Try to find out if relationships with some suppliers are too cosy.*
15. Are standard forms (for example, purchase orders) accompanied with valid terms and conditions used to protect the organizations? *Obtain copies of relevant documentation.*
16. What percentages of purchase orders are issued without a price being listed?
17. Are telephone orders permissible and are they always confirmed in writing?
18. What are the payment terms and are they adhered to?
19. Is the purchasing system fully computerized and integrated with accounts payable?
20. In the interviewee's opinion how good are the computer systems – a help or hindrance?

PURCHASING STRATEGY QUESTIONS

1. Is the area working to a carefully considered purchasing strategy that reflects and is complementary to the organizational strategy?

If so, does the strategy cover areas such as:

• a mission statement;

- commodity analysis and management as a part of the supply chain strategy;
- performance measures;
- agreed and regularly reviewed objectives such as cost savings targets;
- records of past performance to benchmark progress;
- management accountability and organization of staff duties;
- specialist staff and experience requirements;
- growth potential and targets;
- quality of services to be provided;
- operational planning;
- financial data, budgets and accountabilities;
- contingency planning to cover potentially vulnerable areas;
- ongoing marketplace analysis;
- policies and plans for staff development.

PERSONAL QUESTIONS

1. Are they satisfied that their job description adequately records the purchasing duties that they are expected to perform?
2. Has their training for the buying function been satisfactory? *Obtain a list of the training undertaken.*
3. Probe to find out how much knowledge there is on contract law and if there is an awareness of the possible pitfalls of signing contracts that do not adequately protect the organization. *Amateurs may be leaving the organization vulnerable.*
4. Do they have sufficient time to undertake their buying duties satisfactorily? *Can be useful if there is insufficient time to do the job properly as it can be used in future as a reason for the work to be reorganized.*
5. If not, what do they neglect due to time pressures? *More reasons?*
6. Does management understand and appreciate the skills required to be an efficient and effective buyer?
7. Their opinion of the standard and quality of service that the Purchasing Department offers? *Encourage them not to pull any punches.*
8. Would you consider using them?
9. What are the Purchasing Department's strengths and weaknesses?
10. Ask the interviewee what is their preferred negotiating style?
11. What preparations do they make before undertaking an important negotiation?

12. What are their own opinions on accepting the lowest tender, or in what circumstance do they feel that it is beneficial to make value judgements?

13. Do they consider that negotiating tactics are important and if so, which ones do they employ? *Tactics such as bad cop/good cop, mirroring body language or meetings at inconvenient times.*

14. Is cost analysis used as an important negotiating tool? *Broken down costs listed separately such as raw materials, labour, equipment, overheads, delivery and so on.*

15. Ask them to recall examples (facts and figures) of successful negotiations that they have conducted.

16. In their opinion how could purchasing across the organization be improved? *This can be used as a final question to bring the interview to an end on a positive note.*

Aim to wind up the meeting in a friendly and amicable way by thanking the interviewee profusely for their help and co-operation, leaving the door open to return for additional questioning or clarification of the information already received.

Interview notes must be written immediately after the meeting whilst all the subtle detail is fresh in the interviewer's mind. A good method of doing this is to list separately the factual information and subjective opinions. Any summary should also follow the same format. Beware, however, of any recorded information about people falling foul of the Data Protection Act 1998. There are eight guiding principles listed in the Data Protection Act 1998 to make sure that information is handled properly.

The Act says that data must be:

1. fairly and lawfully processed
2. processed for limited purposes
3. adequate, relevant and not excessive
4. accurate
5. not kept for longer than is necessary
6. processed in line with your rights
7. secure
8. not transferred to other countries without adequate protection.

By law, data controllers (your organization will have one) must adhere to the principles listed above. For more information and to read the Data Protection Act 1998 refer to the UK Government website http://www.hmso.gov.uk/acts/acts1998/19980029.htm

A questionnaire should not be considered to be an end in itself because questioning is the very oxygen of a continuing marketing and sales process. Questioning to overcome objections is just as important when opening the door to a new customer as it is to retain an existing customer in perpetuity by constantly asking questions to monitor and understand their changing requirements (needs and wants).

Chapter summary

- Researchers need skill and sensitivity.

- Pick the right mix of questions to suit the level of interviewee.

- Be firm with elusive or unco-operative customers.

- Do not be provoked whatever the circumstances.

- Write up interview notes immediately afterwards.

CHAPTER 10

REVERSE MARKETING

BUYERS BE AWARE

Too many buyers treat suppliers with arrogance and contempt. For instance, they ask for a visit and then keep them waiting ages in reception. Conducting a supplier survey of buyer behaviour should pick up any bad vibes and they should be sorted out promptly and vigorously. Be careful with the preparation of the survey, however, because many suppliers will be reluctant to express criticism for fear of adverse reaction. A carefully worded letter with a follow-up phone call to suppliers will be required to reassure them. Similarly, buyers will need to be persuaded of the benefits of reverse marketing and will need assurance that a supplier survey is not a witch-hunt but is just another step in increasing departmental professionalism. Buyers need to be convinced of the merit of the rule 'always treat suppliers in the same way as you should like to be treated yourself'.

Ignorant buyers don't seem to realize that suppliers have the choice on how they deal with your organization whether it be well, indifferently, badly or not at all. The aim should be that they should like dealing with you, not because you pay over the odds but because you are professional, don't mess them about and that you are 'nice people to do business with'. Sticking to the agreed payment terms also helps. Remember, it is a definite source of competitive advantage if your suppliers treat your organization better than your competitors. Even in my own small business we sort clients into three categories, and I know that we are not unique:

1. **Clients that we enjoy doing business with** and will therefore bend over backwards to help them in any way we can. These are the clients that we will always give priority to. They treat us as equals,

are prepared to work with us to solve problems and always supply clear, unambiguous instructions and specifications.

2. **Clients that we would rather not do business with** if we have plenty of work from category one clients. They often treat us as minions to be constantly at their beck and call. Usually they mess us about because they appear to be disorganized and constantly change their minds. If there is a problem it is always our fault. We therefore spend a great deal of time and effort taking out insurance by confirming every detail in writing. To add insult to injury they usually also keep us waiting for our money.

3. **Clients that we will not do business with.** Late payers – life is too short to spend time chasing money. Clients that are rude and think that they can treat us like serfs. Clients that send out vast, overcomplicated requests for information (RFIs) or requests for quotation (RFQs) full of ridiculous questions that have very little bearing on the job in hand, questions that may be pertinent to our bank manager or accountant but certainly not for revealing to anonymous strangers. They also seem totally unaware of the costs that they are asking us to incur with very little likelihood of any return. Completing their interminable forms can sometimes cost the equivalent of a fee-earning day. Very often we feel that we are being used merely to test the market or provide negotiating ammunition to be employed on their existing supplier or very large rival organizations. We also have a shrewd idea that to protect their own backsides they would never risk using a small supplier anyway. Usually overcomplicated requests are also anonymous, merely mentioning an email address to contact for queries. So if there is no possibility of a personal contact we politely reply thanking them and saying that we are too busy to take on extra work at the moment and then take great delight in shredding their reams of documentation. Local authorities and government departments are the worst culprits, probably paying lip service to government decrees about the importance of supporting small business.

RIGHT WAY/WRONG WAY

Picture the following scenario – a supplier has two important sales meetings on the same day both for similar types of order that he knows is important to both buyers.

Customer meeting (1)

- The buyer keeps the supplier waiting for half an hour in reception and offers scant apology.
- There are no niceties offered, not even a cup of coffee.
- The buyer appears pressed for time, is brusque and appears to want to get the deal done as quickly as possible at the cheapest possible price.
- The buyer pushes hard, insistent on his terms and a deal is struck.
- After a handshake a minion is summoned to see the supplier off the premises.
- The supplier is left with the impression that he has walked into a master/slave relationship.

If the aforesaid buyer had thought for a minute about his actions and placed himself in the supplier's position, outcomes could be very different. As it stands if the supplier needs the business he will knuckle under, but if another buyer comes along later showing more respect the supplier will happily find ways of dumping the account. Meanwhile the supplier will just about comply with the service level agreement but definitely will not put himself out to go the extra mile.

Customer meeting (2)

- The supplier is greeted promptly and warmly on arrival.
- In the relaxed preliminary discussion over a cup of coffee the supplier is given the opportunity to discuss his own agenda.
- The buyer strives to create an atmosphere of trust listing the advantages of dealing with his organization and treats the supplier as an equal.
- The possibility of longer-term arrangements is mooted.
- The supplier obtains the impression that the buyer is firm but fair in their dealings.
- A deal is done that seems to satisfy both parties.
- After a cordial handshake and a walk to reception with the buyer, the supplier is left with the impression that he has made a potentially important business contact.

It does not take a genius to predict which customer will obtain the better quality and service. Obviously in contrast to his customer meeting one, this time the supplier will feel that he will like doing business with this customer and it will be worth providing exceptional service in the hope of building long-term relationships. Both parties have a mutual respect that augurs well for working together to solve any problems that may occur.

This right way/wrong way scenario demonstrates different levels of emotional intelligence displayed by each buyer. Emotional intelligence is a way of describing our capacity for recognizing and understanding our own feelings and relating it to our interpretation of others'. By using this understanding we can build more effective, productive relationships – an important ability for any buyer to develop.

REVERSE MARKETING IN ACTION

Traditionally buyers have tended to remain static awaiting sellers to beat a path to their door. This has been termed transactional buying where the emphasis tends to be upon a single sale and the time horizon tends to be short term. Quality is generally seen to be the concern of production and there tends to be an emphasis on product features and price.

Buyers could afford to be arrogant because when organizations had thousands of suppliers on their book there was no need to treat them half decently because 'there was always another one behind'. However, times have changed and the aim now is to have a small supplier base that are best in class and therefore able to offer competitive advantages to the buyer's organization. It is therefore not very clever to lose a best-in-class supplier by treating them in the old-fashioned typical master/slave manner. More and more organizations are discovering therefore that working with suppliers employing skills jointly to effect continuous improvement is essential to stay ahead of the competition.

Reverse marketing is the technique employed to bring new desirable suppliers on board by broadly adopting the same marketing and selling techniques, as recommended previously. (See Chapter 8, page 81 – Practical Application of Marketing and Sales Theory.) Reverse marketing should also be an integral part of supplier development and supplier relationship (SRM) programmes. The supplier evaluation and rating system described earlier (see Chapter 5, page 49 – Measuring Supplier Performance) is the basis to this and reverse marketing dovetails nicely with the setting up of events such as supplier awards and conferences.

However, this is only the first stage of reverse marketing: it becomes a much deeper issue to companies involved in cutting-edge industries where globalization, technological innovation and speed to market are the principal drivers. In these cases the traditional role of sales people touting their products to buyers has been completely reversed. Now buyers are expected to research and seek out world class suppliers and sell to them the benefits of dealing with the buyer's company. In other situations pricing pressures are forcing buyers to find low labour cost suppliers in developing countries where business practices and cultures are often alien to their own. In these environments Purchasing becomes the catalyst using reverse marketing techniques to locate reliable new sources of supply, implement global delivery chains and form collaborative relationships to ensure continuity. The uncertainties of global trading and longer supply chains also require Purchasing to organize robust contingency arrangements.

The retailing and just-in-time (JIT) manufacturing situations are two obvious areas that are particularly apposite in this regard. JIT manufacturing has proved to be so economical and efficient that it is an increasing trend in production line manufacturing where a relatively standardized product is being produced on a continuous basis, especially if the time between model changes is becoming shorter. Buyers therefore need to seek suppliers whom they will retain for a long period. The main supply criterion being the quality of the goods and reliability of delivery as and when demanded, for in JIT situations down time on the production line as a result of faulty components or late delivery can be very expensive.

When best in class is the driver, not cheap labour, the objective of reverse marketing shifts from merely treating the supplier right to a focus of finding suppliers with matching management structures, policies, IT systems, quality performance, delivery reliability and transparent costing. These functional changes force organizational change in the realization that Purchasing must become more involved in strategic long-term planning and high-level decision making. Progressive organizations working in a global marketplace are therefore finding that the relevant international purchasing expertise and business acumen are vital to the business. Put simply this means that buyers must better understand their suppliers' expectations as well as their own.

Chapter summary

- Arrogant buyers do themselves, their organization and the profession a disservice.

- Suppliers also have choices.

- Treat suppliers in the same way as you would like to be treated.

- Reverse marketing produces results by way of quality and service improvements.

- In a global environment buyers often need to market and sell themselves and their organization to suppliers.

CHAPTER 11

BODY LANGUAGE (NON-VERBAL COMMUNICATION)

DEFINITION

To even raise this subject may seem to fly in the face of the general tenure of a book that thus far has preached a message of objectivity and fact-based analysis. It would be wrong, however, to think that overwhelming logic alone is a sufficiently powerful weapon to win over doubters. However desirable it may be to always remain in control and completely objective, it would be foolish to ignore the fact that it is actually impossible to ignore our own and others' subconscious subjective feelings as we all go about our everyday work. We constantly express our feelings towards others in the form of body language, even if we may be trying to hide or suppress them.

A definition of body language is all non-verbal communication including facial expressions and body movements. These movements and gestures will reveal our true subconscious feelings and may run completely contrary to the actual words being used at the time. It can also include the way we define ourselves in the way of the fashions we wear and ancillary objects we choose. For instance, it would be hardly surprising to receive different reactions from people if we drove a shiny new Rolls Royce one day and a beaten up old banger the next. Similarly to turn up for an interview for a job as a financial adviser at a City bank dressed in an ancient T-shirt and scruffy jeans would not be a wise move, no matter how much we knew about banking. The T-shirt and jeans may, however, be quite appropriate for an interview with a website design creative director, providing they are clean and looking generally new and immaculate.

Humans are social animals that cannot exist without one another and as soon as we are in contact with others of our species we begin communicating. When we use talking as a means of communication we consciously think about the words and sentences we are using but at the same time we also express ourselves with subconscious body movements, sometimes giving out entirely contradictory messages. Often the silent signals that we are giving out and receiving all the time are far more powerful than the spoken word. Some psychologists claim that 93 per cent of emotion is communicated to other people without spoken words. They say that a mere 7 per cent of the impact made on other people depends on what is said, how it is said accounts for 38 per cent and the other 55 per cent is down to body language. This is probably the reason why it is hugely more difficult to persuade someone over the telephone than it is face to face. Video conferencing to some extent is another example, perhaps because only the head and shoulders are seen. It is therefore as well to have some knowledge of the power and effect of body language if we wish to be well received by other people.

MAKING AN IMPACT

It has often been said 'that you never get a second chance to make a good impression' and indeed it has been proven that on first meeting humans form an opinion of each other within ten to sixteen seconds, whether or not anything is said. This first impression is extremely meaningful and once formed difficult to change. Of course most of all this goes on at a subconscious level, although we can feel if we are warming to the other person or not. As it is so important it is worth learning how to use our own body language to good purpose as well as being able to recognise the hidden signals being expressed by others. Bear in mind the complexity involved because it is reckoned that the human body can produce over 700 000 unique body movements, so not even the most expert psychologist can identify them all. Complexity, however, is not an excuse to ignore the most common hidden signals that we employ when communicating with people all of the time.

MEETING AND GREETING

In our business culture people usually greet each other with a handshake and we all have heard jokes about inadequate people with effete limp handshakes, but there is much more to it than that. Handshakes can be strong, soft, firm, short, and long or even sadistically painful.

At the two ends of a scale, aggressive people tend to have firm handshakes where as people with low self-esteem have weak handshakes. You will often see politicians and the like try to exert extra power by also using their other hand to cover the shaking hands or squeezing the other persons elbow, just as they will also try to usher the other person first through a door as a silent proof of their authority. Some men will attempt to domineer women by squeezing their hand in greeting but clever women will move their index finger and little finger in towards the palm to avoid a hand crushing. This also has the effect of negating the dominating effort and showing who really is in control.

Showing an open palm when leading into a handshake is an indication of wishing to convey an impression of trust, sincerity and honesty. A downward facing palm will indicate subconscious feelings of wishing to dominate or be aggressive. When meeting a person for the first time the safest way is to hold the hand upright and vertical as this will indicate equality.

Handshakes are, however, an obvious, visible but not very subtle means of body language communication. They are something that can be easily changed with little effort so why not seek out the opinion of friends and colleagues and practise your handshakes on them? A handshake should convey confidence and professionalism NOT dominance, therefore it needs to be comfortably firm NOT crushing and only others can tell you when it is right.

EYE CONTACT

When star-crossed young lovers gaze longingly into each other's eyes it is a joy to behold and after all it is said that the eyes are the windows on the soul! However, as well as lovers, using our eyes as a means of communication is something that we all constantly employ. Maintaining good eye contact when either talking or listening is an expression of respect and interest in the other person and in our culture we tend to keep eye contact on average for 60 to 70 per cent of the time. People who use their eyes for less than the average or look away may not like you, or perhaps are nervous or shy, or on the other hand feel that their higher status is a justification for ignoring you. Also people who are lying often find it difficult to maintain good eye contact. Conversely someone who is looking you in the eye all of the time is most disconcerting, as staring is perceived to be an aggressive act. Be careful therefore when consciously attempting to improve eye contact with someone you wish to influence.

Wearing sunglasses is a barrier to social contact especially if the people do not know each other very well because obviously the dark lenses greatly reduce the opportunity for eye contact. Some people use them to deliberately hide behind but, whatever the reason, although shades may look trendy they will not greatly help in winning friends and influencing people.

FACIAL EXPRESSIONS

Obviously everybody prefers seeing a smile rather than a frown and when smiles come naturally it makes people feel more at ease with each other and happy. Conversely a frown or wrinkled brow is an indication of confusion, tension or fear. Observe and use the facial expressions of others to measure how the communication is going, upward turns of the mouth are positive signs whereas pursed lips or downward turns of the mouth indicate negative thoughts. Pursing of the lips and twisting them from side to side can also show that thinking is going on or it may even be an attempt to hold back an angry comment. Reading the silent signals will provide early warning signs for you to take corrective action before a relationship turns sour.

POSTURE

Body posture tends to reflect how a person is approaching and feels about a situation. When somebody feels down or disinterested they will be slouched with shoulders drooped or hunched. This applies to either standing or seated positions. Conversely someone whose shoulders are straight with their arms by their side and loosely closed fists inspires confidence that they are interested and ready for action. Also when standing, placing the hands on each side of the waist with the feet apart is an attractive expression of confidence. This is the reason why so many catalogue models are photographed in this pose. Beware, however, of overemphasis, as there is a danger of giving the impression of being of a poser.

Another easy give away is the way that people angle their bodies towards others whom they find interesting or attractive and conversely away from people who do not appeal. It's obvious therefore to identify if someone is friendly or not.

HEAD MOVEMENTS

A confident and self-assured person will signal this by holding their head level both vertically and horizontally. It is also used when people wish to be taken seriously and wish to feel authoritative. To look powerful head movements are kept to a minimum. On the other hand, to show that they are listening and are friendly and receptive the head is tilted to one side or the other continuously. A smile or a grin will often also accompany this head tilting gesture to emphasise the friendly atmosphere being created.

HAND AND ARM GESTURES

Hands are used to emphasize what is said. Pointing at another person is an aggressive act. Political leaders will use pointing or chopping down their hands as a defiant gesture designed to antagonize opponents. Touching a palm to the chest usually indicates an honest comment is being made. The clasping of the hands behind the head whilst leaning back in a chair indicates supreme confidence that will sometimes be taken for arrogance. To show confidence without inspiring antagonism it is better to just touch the fingertips of one hand against the tips of the other to form a steeple shape. This is a favourite for buyers when considering an offer or their next move.

In general, outgoing extrovert people tend to use their arms more in big sweeping movements. This is fine for people they know but it can be off-putting and should therefore be modified for strangers. Arms are great at giving clues at how open and receptive we are to everyone we meet so, when meeting new contacts, it is best to keep arms out to the side of the body or behind the back so as not to appear in any way threatening.

We all cross our arms from time to time, some more than others. It could just be because the temperature is cold but be aware that others generally take it as an expression of disapproval or as an indication of an entrenched position.

LEGS

Leg positions are difficult for us to consciously control, probably because our legs are furthest away from the brain. They tend to move around more when we are stressed, nervous or are being devious. In work or interview situations it is best therefore to attempt to keep legs as still as possible. There are various theories about the way that people cross their legs but just be aware that people who bring their leg up to rest on the knee of another are generally reckoned to be a sign of adopting a defensive position.

TOUCHING

In this world of ever-increasing political correctness this may appear to be a delicate aspect of body language that is too fraught to tackle. Indeed as a society we do not encourage bodily contact because it can so easily be misconstrued as being of a sexual nature. However, touching in the right way can have a very powerful impact in aiding communication. There is a famous experiment where a librarian was asked to touch or not touch the hand of readers as they handed over their library cards. When the readers were subsequently questioned it was discovered that the ones who had been touched on the hand thought that service provided by the librarian was much better than the ones who had not been touched.

A light touch therefore on the arm, shoulder or back when giving advice, an order, asking a favour, trying to persuade or listening to the worries of others will greatly reinforce the message we are seeking to convey.

INVASION OF PERSONAL SPACE

One of the most insincere people I know happens to be a relative – by marriage. Whenever I meet her she tends to stand with her nose about twelve inches from mine, stare me straight in the eye and mutter platitudes that she thinks I would like to be hearing. Her demeanour is both off-putting and disturbing, especially as I do also know that she is a terrible gossip and will be bad-mouthing me just as soon as my back is turned. Perhaps she is very short-sighted and is too vain to wear glasses or contact lenses but I doubt it.

The distance that you stand or sit from others is therefore crucial to creating a favourable impression. Too close, like my dear relative, is considered pushy or in modern parlance 'in your face'. However, too far away can indicate keeping your distance or even being standoffish. A good indicator is that if you notice that as you move closer to someone they back away then you are invading their personal space and upsetting their comfort zone.

The poet W.H. Auden summed it up as follows:

Some thirty inches form my nose
The frontier of my person goes
And all the untilled land between
Is private pages and demesne.
Yo stranger unless with bedroom eyes
I beckon you to fraternise,
Beware of ever crossing it.
I have no gun but I can spit!

However, watch out for some pushy sales people who will deliberately lean all over a buyer's desk in a blatant invasion of space in an attempt to intimidate and dominate when they are desperate to clinch a sale. It is not advisable to spit but you can express disapproval by cutting short the discussion and dismissing them.

THE ART OF LISTENING

It has been said that as we have two ears and only one mouth we should be using the former twice as much as the latter. People who listen twice as much as they talk come over as good communicators who are good at holding balanced conversations. The problem is that when we are nervous or ill at ease we either cannot think of anything to say or talk far too much – usually about ourselves. Listening to the other person is the key and then responding by asking questions that encourage them to talk about themselves is guaranteed to create a favourable impression. The art of listening is so vitally important in any human contact situation that a full checklist is supplied below.

1. **Courtesy**. Be polite to the other person. It is rude to ignore their point of view, interrupt or upstage.
2. **Taking turns**. Let the other person express their point of view first. This can be of advantage because they may reveal clues about their real wants and needs that you can subsequently tailor the discussion to address. Given scope the other person may even solve your perceived problem for you.
3. **It is almost impossible to talk and listen at the same time**. It may, however, be possible to observe body language when talking in order to change tack if negative vibes are observed. In general conversation, people interrupt each other all the time by butting

in when there is the slightest pause. However, we all hate being interrupted because it disturbs thought patterns so, if wishing to make a favourable impression, it is polite to let the other person finish the point that they are making first.

4.   **Identify the main theme**. Often a number of irrelevant points will be mentioned merely to add to the speaker's comfort zone. Take advantage of the fact that you can think quicker than the other person can talk so constantly ask yourself questions such as – 'What is the real point they are trying to make?' 'What do they really expect of me?' 'What are there real wants and needs?'. You will then be in a position to give positive feedback and understanding when it is your turn to talk.

5.   **Ignore distractions**. Train yourself to ignore them because therwise they will affect your conversation. Office noise, an ugly tie, dirty carpets do not really matter – concentrating on what is being said does.

6.   **Take notes**. First of all ask politely if it is in order because, unless you have a super memory, brief notes of the important bits of the conversation may prove invaluable later. They must, however, be brief because you cannot listen and take detailed notes at the same time. Review them immediately after the meeting to ensure they make sense.

7.   **Objectivity**. React to the message being given out and not to the person however objectionable, unpleasant and even rude they may be. Understanding the message gives advantage if planning to fight another day.

8.   **Body language**. Listen and watch for the hidden signals to judge the emotional messages being given. Feelings may sometimes be a nuisance but are important. For instance, judge what they are really implying or why that is being said in that way.

9.   **Feedback**. Constantly check your understanding of the situation by asking meaningful questions at the right time. Make sure you really hear what is being said not what you want to hear. Repeat your understanding of their reply and give time for further comment.

10.   **Questions**. Ask open-ended questions to elicit useful responses. Yes or no answers are not helpful except to confirm a fact. Questions like 'What do *you* think is a possible solution?' or 'Where do *we* go from here?' will force the speaker to enlarge on the subject.

11. **Selectivity**. Try to sort the wheat (useful information) from the chaff (irrelevant conversation). React to or memorize only the salient points.
12. **Relaxation**. Try to put the other person at their ease by creating a relaxing friendly environment, even if underneath you may feel nervous or apprehensive.
13. **Criticism**. Do not be too critical of the other's point of view. Be patient and do not react emotionally or, worse still, lose your temper. Keep an open mind and listen to their point of view as you can always come back with a rational counter-argument later.
14. **Attention**. Demonstrate your interest by nodding your head, leaning slightly forward, giving the right amount of eye contact and muttering the occasional word of agreement and encouragement.
15. **Evaluation**. After every important meeting score yourself on the result based on your strengths and weaknesses. If a colleague is also present ask them for feedback on your performance. Most of all keep learning from your mistakes because the art of listening is a life skill that we can all benefit from being better at if we are going to make the most of any relationship.

SPOTTING A LIE

Honesty is the best policy but we all tell lies at times even if they are only white ones designed to avoid hurting the feelings of others. However, it is especially beneficial for buyers to be able to spot when someone is lying because even the best suppliers are inclined to tell us 'porkies' when they are in trouble. Unfortunately we cannot subject them to a polygraph lie-detecting machine. However, even the law authorities that do have access to this equipment often also use video interviews to back up lie-detecting machine evidence with simultaneous evaluation of body language.

Typically when someone is lying they are described as having shifty eyes because they are avoiding eye contact. They may also subconsciously cover their mouth and speak through their fingers or rub their eyes when talking. Another give away is covering or poking a finger into their ears. More subtle gestures that need close observation are a nose wrinkle as if there is a nasty smell about or a slight downward curl at the corners of the mouth.

MIRRORING

When people like each other and are holding a mutually agreeable conversation they tend to naturally reflect each other's body movements. This is called mirroring and is a technique that is often deliberately and ruthlessly employed by well trained sales people. Firstly they will deliberately mirror any favourable body language that the buyer uses then move subtly to get the buyer to mirror their own positive postures before leading them to close the sale. However, if they spot negative gestures such as the buyer covering their mouth, touching their nose or near an eye they will realize that the prospect is withdrawing and therefore another tack is required to bring them back to a more favourable position.

Tests have been undertaken with leaders talking to small groups and it has been proven that the speakers who mirror positive body language exhibited by the group as against ones who do not will be thought of as being more successful, appealing and friendly by their listeners.

GENDER AND CULTURAL DIFFERENCES

Women's intuition is a powerful ability that should not be ignored and is probably a result of being better than men at subconsciously interpreting body language. Science says that this is because women can process messages simultaneously in both their right and left brains. For instance, women are much better at quickly and instinctively knowing if someone is not being sincere or is lying. The trouble is that often they do not follow their instincts, as they tend to form just as many disastrous relationships as men do!

Children absorb non-verbal communication at the same time as they learn to talk. Be aware therefore just as words are different in different countries and cultures, so is body language. For instance, in Greece it is a very rude gesture to hold up the palm of the hand in front of someone else. UK body language will therefore not necessarily work in other cultures; just like the spoken word, translation will be necessary if misunderstandings are to be avoided.

IS THE STUDY OF BODY LANGUAGE WORTHWHILE?

Inevitably there will be some cynics who will dismiss the theory of body language as being just another piece of psychological mumbo jumbo. To the cynics I say try measuring its effectiveness with an experiment of attempting to hold a meaningful conversation with someone whilst keeping your eyes shut all the time. Most people will be forced to admit that their level of understanding inevitably is hampered. This is the reason why it is often more difficult to make yourself understood on the telephone than it is face to face. Whenever people meet and talk, non-verbal communication will also be going on, whether you happen to think it is important or not. It is not the be-all and end-all of understanding or influencing someone else but it is as well to realize that it is a key component of human interaction. Therefore if buyers wish to effectively sell their services to others in the organization they would be foolish to ignore its potential power.

THE POSITIVE APPLICATION OF BODY LANGUAGE

Most of us would like to make ourselves more attractive to and better liked by others. Let us therefore consider the practical application of some of the positive aspects of body language which are easy to use in everyday situations.

- Approach as close as possible without invading another's space or causing embarrassment.
- Make plenty of eye contact.
- Appear positive by adopting a smiling, warm, friendly manner.
- Stand up straight with shoulders straight and chin out. When seated lean back slightly to encourage informality but when listening lean forward to show that you are interested in what is being said.
- Use single and double head nods to demonstrate understanding and appreciation of what is being said to you.
- Make expressive open gestures without overdoing it.
- Dress according to the group norm but try to add a splash of colour to make a little additional impact.
- Touch as much as is appropriate and acceptable and encourage touching from others.
- Try to talk and listen in equal proportions. Do not talk too quickly and adjust voice volume to suit the situation.
- When the conversation is starting to go well try mirroring the positive movements of the other person to increase the good vibes.

THE VOICE

There are certain aspects of voice communication that are non-verbal. For instance volume, pitch and tone. We tend to prefer smooth low tones to screeching voices. It is said that Margaret Thatcher, when first elected Prime Minister, deliberately trained herself to speak in a much lower tone. Surely many of the Blair babes (new female MPs in the Tony Blair administration) have taken the same lesson excessively to heart to the extent that some sound very butch indeed. On the same subject it is interesting to muse whether a popular politician like Ann Widdecombe would have become leader of the Conservative Party if the pitch of her voice had been different.

In one-to-one conversations with people we know we can often get away with the excessive use of 'er, ah, um' or the footballer's favourite in interview 'you know' to cover gaps as we struggle to produce the next word. However, when addressing an audience it can be excruciating and should be avoided as much as possible.

Chapter summary

- We cannot afford to ignore the importance of non-verbal communication in influencing human relationships.

- Body language will often reveal what the other person is really thinking.

- An understanding of body language will make us better communicators.

- Subconscious feelings about another person are formed very quickly.

- Reading the subconscious signs enables corrective action to be undertaken when things are going wrong.

CHAPTER 12

TECHNOLOGY COMES TO OUR AID

THE RIGHT SYSTEM

Most companies are working hard to increase market share by maximising their competitive advantage in every area. However, as I have said previously in this book, many are missing a trick because their management of the supply side is weak. Expenditure on products and services is always considerable, often amounting to 60 to 80 per cent of total expenditure, dwarfing for instance salary costs. The reason for missing this trick is that often buying accountability is fragmented with a lack of management information, resulting in no one at board level taking active responsibility for buying and the supply side.

Of course this does not apply everywhere for instance the automotive, large retail and supermarket market sectors run superefficient buying operations. What then is required to match the best-in-class approach of these sectors? Firstly there is a need to understand how much money is being spent, who is spending it, on what and with which suppliers? This is often easier said than done because the computer systems to gather and analyse this information may not be in position. It can therefore be a painstaking process to gather the figures to form the basis for top management to take strategic decisions and institute change. Their focus must be to ensure that the business is buying high value at low cost on a measured, consistent basis, with the objective of contributing to both increased competitive advantage and bottom line contribution. This does not mean centralized buying but in order to strike the best deals it does need to be centre led.

Can the use of technology provide an alternative way to solve all the problems? Well, no – but the right computer system can gather relevant management information in real time and thus be the catalyst to ensure that the beneficial changes are introduced. A fully integrated computer system is the ideal. Integrated means the ability for the system to interact with internal customers, suppliers and of course finance, especially accounts payable.

Also much of the drudgery of buying administration paperwork is heaven sent for handling by efficient computer systems, leaving buyers free to spend more time on the elements of the job that really matter.

In practice, however, computer systems for purchasing all too often come way down the top management wish list or they are tagged onto a finance system as an afterthought. There are plenty of very good purchasing systems available but some that are sold as a finance package with the possibility of tagging on an additional purchasing module are very poor because all the programming effort and expertise has initially been expended on getting the financial workings right. It is therefore vitally important that Purchasing management are involved in a systems instalation from the very outset in the design, specification, build and testing of programmes. Purchasing must be working at every stage as a decision-making senior partner if a practical, workable system is to be installed. All software must also be web enabled to take full advantage of eCommerce opportunities.

A BEGINNER'S GUIDE TO eCOMMERCE

To date, despite Government exhortations, the take-up of eCommerce in the purchasing process has been painfully slow. Therefore, at the risk of teaching some granny how to suck eggs, an eCommerce guide follows in order to reinforce some of the advantages it offers, not least that it can be used as part of the unique perceived benefit (UPB) marketing offer.

eCommerce can be used to manage and action at every stage of the purchasing process from sourcing through buying and payment to contract management and will include:

- eSourcing covering the contractual process including eRFIs, eRFQs and reverse auctions.
- eProcurement organizing the transactional processes such as eTenders, orders and contracts plus new techniques like the use of customised eCatalogues and marketplaces.
- ePayment including invoicing, payment and the use of corporate purchasing credit cards.

Reverse auctions are a powerful new tool presenting exciting opportunities for companies to substantially reduce procurement costs. The way reverse auctions work is that you decide on a suitable product or service, prepare and publish a detailed specification and invite suppliers to attend your internet auction. Name the date and time, usually no more than a couple of hours, and sit back and watch suppliers beat one another up on price. The prices are posted up for all to see as they come in but the suppliers names are coded so only you know who they actually are.

You can expect auctions to generate substantial cost savings but the process needs careful managing. There are three ways to set up the auction procedure.

1. An IT department can write the programme – but they would be reinventing the wheel.
2. The software can be purchased to integrate with your existing systems – could be expensive.
3. You can use a third party specialist to run auctions on your behalf – an excellent low cost way to kick start the learning curve.

Usually savings of at least 20 per cent will be achieved. Recent auctions with companies in the retail sector have delivered savings of over 30 per cent within weeks rather than months and on a range of spend categories from services to goods for resale.

Mark Hopton, Senior Partner, KPMG.

Successfully-run reverse auctions have achieved savings in the order of:

- vehicle leasing: saving 18 per cent;
- office supplies: savings of 24 per cent;
- personal protection equipment: saving 22 per cent;
- human resources: savings of up to 70 per cent!;
- CNC drilled components: saving 12 per cent;
- maintenance, repair and operations equipment: savings of 21 per cent;
- building materials: saving 14 per cent.

USE OF ONLINE AUCTIONS

Online auctions have been used for:

- obtaining new commodities or services;
- renewing existing contracts;
- offering new consolidated spend opportunities;
- buying significant spot purchases;
- benchmarking and awarding contracts for frequently tendered commodities and services.

Advantages for buyers

The advantages for buyers of online auctions are:

- transparency. Enables you to find out what the real market price is, maybe for the first time;
- drives competition amongst suppliers – and how!;
- quick, efficient and paperless method of buying;
- can identify efficient new suppliers;
- an alternative new practical tool;
- cut costs, saves money;
- they can make Purchasing a star in top management eyes!

Advantages for suppliers

The advantages for suppliers of online auctions are:

- for inefficient suppliers – not a lot because the process sorts out the men from the boys;
- transparency – suppliers are able to benchmark themselves against the marketplace;
- efficient, best in class suppliers will obtain more business.

ACTION PLAN

The following action plan is recommended:

- Just like negotiation, the more you put into the preparation the better the result.
- Only invite suppliers you would confidently use. There must be at least three, preferably more.
- Select something in which price makes up at least 25 per cent of the decision-making process

- A decent amount of money has to be involved, say £50 000 and upwards.
- It is important to effectively sell your auction plan to suppliers. Your objective is to obtain their commitment.
- Suppliers need to be light on their feet to win at an auction so they will also need to plan thoroughly to be able to maintain the commercial flexibility that an auction demands.
- Commercially inept suppliers will ruin the process.
- Will you necessarily award the contract to the lowest bid? If not, you have a subtle problem preparing your suppliers.
- Have a technical helpline up and running to sort out queries as they arise.
- Obtain a senior management champion to drive the changes in organizational culture required.
- Use the process to market purchasing expertise, invite Board members to watch the process live.
- Follow up with all suppliers so that everyone keeps learning.
- Resist the temptation of bidding yourself to encourage a lower price.
- It is very helpful to all parties if suppliers also understand eCommerce and reverse auctions. This is why it pays to also organize training for them if necessary.

The *Strategic Procurement Review 2004* published by Market Focus Research revealed that only 13 per cent of respondents have a fully implemented eCommerce strategy so there must be enormous scope for progressive organizations to grab the 20 per cent savings and place themselves in pole position.

Reverse auctions are highlighted here because they can be a formidable part of a marketing UPB offer. Maverick buyers in the main have not as yet latched on to using them. They are easily presented as exciting and dynamic events so invite Board members and key decision makers to attend. They cannot fail to be impressed.

A final word of caution: reverse auctions are not an end in themselves; they are merely an effective additional tool in the buyers' armoury. They have developed a bad reputation in some quarters: witness some Luddite supplier organizations that are advising their members not to participate. The large savings are often a one-off – you cannot expect to continually save 20 per cent on the same commodity.

Chapter summary

- It is impossible to effectively manage purchasing expenditure without an efficient integrated computer system.

- Purchasing must be in charge of choosing the right computer system.

- eCommerce has a tremendous future.

- Reverse auctions can make the function a star with top management.

CHAPTER 13

ETHICS

REPUTATION IS ALL

It is absolutely vital for purchasing people to maintain and be seen to maintain a reputation for absolute integrity in all business matters. Without the credibility of a scrupulously honest reputation it is pointless to attempt to market and sell the function.

MEASURING BUYER HONESTY

This is a very difficult area because if one 'bad apple' is employed and subsequently exposed it can in an instant destroy years of hard work in building a trusted and respected reputation for procurement staff in particular and the purchasing profession in general. However, short of employing regular lie-detector tests on staff, one can never be absolutely sure of exactly what is going on within buyer/seller relationships. Over the years many high profile fraud cases have come to court involving purchasing staff often at a very senior level. Are these cases rare or only the tip of the iceberg? So how many buyers are regularly on the take, maybe only fraudulently pocketing small sums of money or benefits in kind? Are they getting away with it? It is impossible to know, but there are many sensible precautions that can be taken to make life difficult for the odd 'bad apple' buyer.

Over the past few years I have conducted many buyer recruitment interviews on behalf of the clients of the recruitment division of the Chartered Institute of Purchasing & Supply (CIPS) and it is always important to probe ethical standards. A standard question is to ask, 'What is your opinion about buyers accepting bottles of alcohol or other gifts from suppliers at Christmas?' I have always been surprised when only a minority give the answer that the Institute itself recommends to its members that 'buyers should only accept gifts of small intrinsic value such as a diary or calendar'. Frequently I have been given answers such as 'we share them out equally among all members of the department' or 'we raffle them internally' or 'we give the odd bottle to friendly internal customers' or 'the boss grabs most of it'. It always makes me wonder whether they ever stop to consider who really bears the cost of all the Christmas largesse: do they honestly think that it is the supplier? They should also consider the feelings of resentment and perhaps even jealousy that colleagues in other departments feel when they see bottles of booze pile up in reception for collection by purchasing department staff. In January it will take this same purchasing staff a great deal of sales and marketing effort to overcome the December gossip about 'our buyers being on the take again'!

Can we draw a line between acceptable and unacceptable inducements that suppliers tend to offer buyers? And why is it seldom the other way around? To answer the quastions we need to strip the buyer/seller relationship bare in an attempt to establish principles and ground rules to help protect basically honest buyers from unscrupulous sellers, whilst at the same time protecting employers from naïve or greedy buyers. Those of us involved in buying and selling for a living know just how competitive the clinching of an order for a supplier can be in today's cut-throat environment. Similarly we realize how hard it must be for suppliers to make a profit under these circumstances. Why then will a seller give away to the buyer some of that hard won profit by offering entertainment, free travel, buyer hospitality or gifts? Of course a buyer will always claim that the acceptance of inducements will not influence the choice of supplier decision in the slightest – *nonsense!* Inducements cost the supplier in the form of reduced profit. The reason they are offered is to try to beat the competition by unfairly distorting, influencing or eroding the impartiality of the buying decision-making process.

Inducements equals unfair influence equals *bribery* or purchasing fraud. There is no such thing as a free lunch so the buyer's employer one way or another will find that they finish up paying extra for company goods and services. Mintel estimate that the corporate hospitality industry in the UK alone is worth £700 million per annum. That is nearly £20 a year for every British adult, and we have the cheek to criticize other countries where backhanders are more obvious. Does it make sense for £700 million to be voluntarily removed from supply side bottom line, £700 million that could be better employed by being invested in increasing the efficiency and world competitiveness of UK industry?

To effect change the first protection that organizations employing staff to buy on their behalf can make is to introduce an *ethical code*. Maybe our politicians should also take note: their codes seem fairly weak and they appear to be pretty good at accepting freebies such as holidays in Tuscany? Despite Parliament having a declaration of interest policy, regular scandals would appear to indicate that it does not work very well in practice.

DEVISING AN ETHICAL CODE

This draft can of course be modified slightly to suit most circumstances:

Universal principles

Staff shall never use their authority for personal gain and shall seek to uphold the standing and reputation of the organization by:

- Maintaining impeccable standards of integrity in all their business relationships both inside and outside the company.
- Optimizing the use of resources for which they are responsible to provide the maximum benefit to the company.
- Complying both with the letter and the spirit of the law of the United Kingdom and the European Community.
- Adhering to guidance on professional practice that may be issued by management from to time.
- Complying with the company's contractual obligations.

Ethical guidance

- **Declaration of interest**. Any personal interest which may impinge or might reasonably be deemed by others to impinge on impartiality in any matter relevant to his or her duties must be declared (for example, share ownership or buying from relations). A buyer should not have any personal interest in any supplier with whom business is being conducted.
- **Confidentiality and accuracy of information**. The confidentiality of information received in the course of work should be respected and should never be used for personal gain. Information given in the course of work should be true and fair and never designed to mislead.
- **Competition**. While bearing in mind the advantage to the company of maintaining continuing relationships with some suppliers, any

arrangements that might in the long term prevent operation of fair competition should be avoided.

- **Business gifts**. Only items of very small intrinsic value such as business diaries or calendars should be accepted at any time.
- **Hospitality**. There are sometimes occasions when the networking opportunities can be an advantage. However, business entertainment must always be pre-approved by line management and only accepted if the buyer's organization is prepared to reciprocate to the same value.
- **Business dining/lunches**. The word 'business' is the key because the informal atmosphere of dining or lunch meetings can sometimes be beneficial. However, dining should never be purely social and should be kept to modest proportions. In order that the buyer should never be in a position of feeling beholden to the supplier, the organization must also be prepared to fund the buyer to reciprocate equally.
- **Supplier visits**. Business trips to visit the supply sources or manufacturing units are often a vital part of the supplier selection process. However, to emphasize the business nature of the trip, the buyer should not allow the seller to pay travel or subsistence costs.
- **Hospitality recording**. Records of dining, hospitality and supplier visits must be maintained and approved by line management. Verification will be a part of the internal audit process.
- **Compliance**. Copies of the organization's ethical code will be signed and dated by all persons involved in buying goods and services on behalf of the organization to acknowledge understanding, acceptance and commitment to all aspects of the code. A signed copy will be held on the person's personnel file. Non-compliance will result in disciplinary action including dismissal being taken.

INTER-DEPARTMENTAL AND INTERNATIONAL DIFFERENCES

In organizations that introduce ethical codes for procurement, buyers will often complain that it is not fair because their own sales force are still offering all sorts of goodies to their clients. This is a tricky management problem that is best tackled head-on. It should be pointed out that, irrespective of the sales situation, the ethical code demonstrates the professional approach of the purchasing team by taking a lead in demonstrating the advantages of adopting a morally unassailable approach to business ethics. Despite appearing two-faced, sadly in such cases there appears to be no alternative to the organization maintaining a Chinese wall.

Looking globally, the problems of corruption take on nightmare proportions where bribery in some countries is an endemic way of life in every strata of society. As mere purchasers we can do very little about this except to promote upfront, clear, unequivocal high standards in all our international business dealings. However, it must be extremely difficult for our sales colleagues to even get a foothold in some markets without resorting to practices that would be wholly unacceptable in most Western countries. It is also a very risky business: for instance, in 2005 the US chemical giant Monsanto agreed to pay a fine of $1.5 million for bribing a high-level Indonesian official in the environmental ministry in 2002. At the time Monsanto was facing stiff opposition from activists against its plans for introducing genetically engineered cotton into Indonesia. The $50 000 bribe was designed to avoid environmental impact studies taking place on its cotton. To add insult to injury, despite acceptance of the bribe, the official still did not authorize the waiving of the environmental study.

With regard to the UK, it is a trifle uncomfortable to realize that we are certainly not top of the league with regard to buyer honesty. Transparency International publishes a league table on bribery acceptance based on a scale of one to ten with a score of ten indicating the lowest bribe rate. Top of the league come Australia, Sweden and Switzerland, all with a score of eight. Next come the UK, Germany and Singapore with a score of six. Followed by France and USA with a score of five. In descending order the business sectors with the highest incidence of bribery are:

- public works and construction
- arms and defence
- oil and gas
- property
- telecoms
- power generation and transmission.

The source of this information, Transparency International, is a non-governmental organization that monitors corruption, especially between the private sector and government officials. Focusing on the economic rather than the moral costs of corruption, it publishes the authoritative and widely quoted 'Bribe Payers Index'. For more information go to www.transparency.org

If as part of our marketing offer we present Purchasing as being the ideal guardians of best practice business ethics, it is as well that we know of the weaknesses that exist in our society. For instance, the Organisation for Economic Co-operation and Development (OECD) published in March 2005 an extensive review of how the UK is implementing the OECD's anti-bribery convention. The review was particularly critical on the lack of prosecutions in the UK for bribery of foreign officials by UK companies; the lack of clarity over who should deal with enforcement of alleged crimes; and the lack of resources for the police to investigate and prosecute them. According to The Corner House (www.thecornerhouse.or.uk), a not-for-profit company dedicated to supporting democratic and community movements for environmental and social justice, this prompted a prominent group of NGOs and trade unions to call on the government to take prompt action. It reads as follows:

> *In light of the highly critical OECD report on the UK's implementation of the OECD Convention on Combating Bribery, the undersigned trade unions and non-governmental organizations call for the UK Government to take immediate action to meet its international commitments on bribery and corruption. If the UK Government is serious about tackling global poverty during its leadership of the G8 and EU, and making a real difference to Africa, then it must demonstrate its commitment by taking urgent action to combat bribery by UK companies abroad. The UK Government has a unique opportunity in 2005 to show political will on tackling corruption by implementing the OECD report's recommendations as quickly and as thoroughly as possible. The recent Commission for Africa report highlighted the devastating impacts of corruption on development in Africa. It called for developed countries to combat corruption among their businesses working in Africa. Despite numerous international anti-corruption conventions, it said, the persistence of corruption suggested that these conventions were not being enforced. 'It is time the international community turned words into action', it stated. This OECD report shows that the UK is among the developed countries that have yet to 'turn words into action'.*

So no room for complacency though one hesitates to take the gloomy view expressed by a northern Chief Constable who once famously said '5 per cent of people are incorruptible, 5 per cent are totally corrupt. The rest are just waiting for the right opportunity.'

ETHICAL POLICY IN PRACTICE

Wal-Mart, possibly the most successful retailer in the world, has a corporate culture that includes flying economy, sharing hotel rooms and *not* accepting even a can of Coke from a supplier. Sam Walton the founder of Wal-Mart said:

The customer gets no benefit out of the buyer having a nice bottle of wine at dinner. In many ways it is the customer that is subsidising the entertainment, the trip to the US Open or the Super Bowl or the cruise. Whatever it is, the customer is paying for it.

Some would be uncomfortable (literally) with Wal-Mart's travel policy but can anyone disagree that they are dead right on the subject of entertainment?

Within my own experience I must confess that I have not always been a convert to the philosophy that buyers must never accept gifts except items of small intrinsic value such as diaries or calendars. My conversion occurred one October many years ago when I was Purchasing Manager responsible for several different commodity-buying teams. When walking the floor one day I was on my way to welcome back a lady buyer who had just returned from maternity leave. However, before I arrived at her desk I could hear her talking from behind the open plan screening to her buying team colleagues saying, 'Christmas is coming so my first job will be to make sure that all the suppliers know I'm back.' I must confess that this wholly unprofessional attitude really made me see red and I immediately turned on my heel to return to my office and start to rewrite and considerably tighten up our ethical code. However, when I had calmed down I decided that its immediate introduction would be unwise because it might cause resentment and embarrassment for both suppliers and staff. The new code was therefore introduced in the following February with meetings to explain the new policy to our staff and an explanatory letter to all suppliers. It appeared to be well received by everybody and by the next October it was pleasing to overhear the odd phone conversation of buyers explaining to suppliers that our professional ethical code did not allow for the acceptance of Christmas gifts. Buyer's Christmas perks then became part of history!

THE PSYCHOLOGY OF A FRAUDSTER

I have often wondered why a very small minority of individuals risk shame, degradation and their job by defrauding their employer. Can it be worth it? Many would say 'yes, but only for many million pounds and a life of millionaire luxury'. However, I remember the Personnel Director at Abbey National telling me inevitably in a business that handled mountains of cash, he had sacked many people for fraud. He said 'yes, a few had stolen hundreds of thousands of pounds but the majority had been sacked for small items such as fiddling their expenses'. To me this is completely baffling but nevertheless is a phenomenon that cannot be ignored, especially in a purchasing environment where there can be many temptations on offer for the weak or unworldly. According to a MORI poll commissioned in 2005 by a consortium of insurers, business fraud costs the UK over £550 million per annum. This may well be the tip of the iceberg because presumably the organizations polled could only report on the fraud that had been uncovered.

Is there anyway of telling if a buyer is liable to temptation? Well, there may be some sophisticated psychological tests available that would spot a trait but to put buyers through such a test would probably trample all over their human rights. In my experience it is very difficult to spot a crafty fraudster by their behaviour except by having very tight procedures in place that make segregation of duties and effective audit trails a high priority. Whilst working in Abbey National my Group Purchasing unit performed an excellent marketing and sales job on the Marketing Division by persuading them to hand over most of their procurement to us. There were however, some exceptions, for instance, we found it very difficult to break into the area that offered marketing promotions despite us knowing that we could buy better by dealing direct with suppliers form the Pacific rim rather than continue to use UK agencies. The area was managed by a very bright young university graduate who was ranked number three in the Marketing Department, a high-flyer destined for the top. In addition he had a winning personality liked by all including myself. Members of my staff and I had been to see him on numerous occasions to sell the expertise of the purchasing team but were always fobbed off with promises that as soon as their existing contracts expired he would certainly hand over the work. As I was on the point of taking matters up with the Marketing Director I was surprised to hear that the aforesaid Marketing Promotions Manager had been marched off the premises by security staff and sent on indefinite gardening leave. Subsequently in court it came out that he had been in collusion with the directors of a couple of agencies and had defrauded the company of over £2 million and was sent to prison for four years. No one had ever suspected and despite regular independent internal and external audits he had got away with it for some time. The only way he was caught was that a disgruntled member of his own staff became suspicious of the number of apparently duplicate invoices that he was approving and reported him. There was much discussion at the time of why a very bright personable individual with the world at his feet should throw it all away in such a reckless manner. There was just one silver lining: we did obtain control of the marketing promotion procurement.

As a profession, however, we are living in a glass house as regards corruption and therefore cannot afford to throw stones. One famous case in 1994 involved a Ministry of Defence Procurement Director who was sent to jail for four years for accepting bribes for £2.25 million from just three companies. But it did not end there because it was estimated at the time that the true cost of this bribery to the Government due to increased costs from distortion of the market amounted to some £200 million. It all goes to prove that the most unlikely of individuals can undertake procurement fraud and the only defence to mitigate against the problem is firstly to have effective procedures and controls in place and secondly to remain constantly aware and vigilant.

COMMON SENSE PRECAUTIONS FOR BUYERS AND MANAGERS

A list of common sense precautions for buyers and managers follows:

- Avoid giving the impression of favouring any supplier by spending too much time with any one in particular.
- Be wary of forming close friendships with suppliers. There is a strong possibility that you will be used. Witness the buyers that are disappointed when they change jobs to buying new products and never see their old sales rep. 'friends' again.
- Friendships with suppliers can also damage the organization. Suppliers will tend to think that they have buyer friends in their pocket and may therefore become complacent and give other more demanding buyers priority when they face production or delivery problems.
- Always declare any socialising outside working hours. It is most unwise to arrange dinner parties with suppliers either in your home or theirs.
- Try to move buyers around, do not leave with them working with one set of commodities and suppliers for too long. Too long in one area also does nothing for their training and development needs.
- Business lunch meetings can be useful places to gather intelligence on suppliers and the market place. However, ensure that buyers never feel beholden by providing the means for them to pick up the tab 50 per cent of the time.
- Watch out for buyers who regularly fix midday or close of play meetings with suppliers. They may be taking their turn at paying for their round at the pub – but you never know.

- Do not cut corners on procedures particularly in the areas of segregation of duties and supplier approval. There have been innumerable cases of purchasing fraud when buyers have managed to add a close relation to the approved supplier list.
- Watch out for buyers who appear to be living life styles above their means, are gamblers or have an excessive debt burden. Unscrupulous suppliers may target them for 'help'.
- Bearing in mind that dishonest suppliers can be very subtle when making dubious approaches to buyers, the slightest suspicion should always be reported to senior management.
- Listen to the marketplace grapevine, reps love the whiff of scandal.
- Make it known that, all things being equal, suppliers that aspire to the same ethical standards will be favoured.
- Watch out for specifications being slanted to suit one supplier.
- Be suspicious of loaded terms and conditions that will automatically preclude a number of suppliers.
- Above all, do not sweep the possibility of fraud under the carpet but encourage regular departmental discussion on the subject. Being open and frank about all aspects of business ethics is the best defence against temptations, backed up of course with a policy that buyers on the take will always be sacked and will probably never work anywhere near purchasing again.

CONTROLS

As mentioned under the list of precautions, the principal control weapon against corruption and fraud is segregation of duties. There are a number of control points that therefore need tackling:

- Authorization to purchase. Who decides that there is a buying requirement and is responsible for the requisition/specification process?
- Supplier selection. Who decides which suppliers are approached, undertakes the negotiation and recommends the supplier to be used?
- Purchase order/Contract authority. Who approves the deal, supplier choice and counter signs the order?
- Goods received notes. Who checks what has been delivered matches the order for specification and quantity?

- Payment. Who checks the invoice against the purchase order (PO) and the goods received note (GRN) and instigates action in the event of mismatch?

As a minimum requirement The Chartered Institute of Purchasing & Supply (CIPS) recommends that at least two people are delegated to take responsibility at each of the following stages:

- determining the need to buy, including specification and budget implication;
- undertaking the purchase including sourcing and supplier choice;
- financial aspects including invoice matching and payment authorization.

For some organizations goods receipt is also a critical area where segregation of duty controls are essential to avoid shrinkage in all its many varied forms occurring.

As a vital part of any formal written procurement procedures, there is a requirement for a list to be drawn up of the decision-making limits (mainly financial) for the staff that are authorized to make the decisions at each stage. It should be published by way of delegated authorities against names with sample signatures. Remember the requirement for a second signature must not be merely a rubber stamping exercise. The second signature is not fulfilling their responsibility unless they rigorously challenge and probe the decisions they are being asked to approve. Make second signature authorities aware that if they are not conscientious and something goes amiss they are likely to be accused of collusion.

Constant monitoring of adherence to the ethical code and rotation of duties where possible should also be carried out.

WHISTLE-BLOWING

It is unfortunate that whistle-blowing has received a bad press in some quarters because of some highly publicised political cases where the whistle-blower has ended up by being persecuted by the very organization against which help was being offered. However, used properly it can be a source for rooting out corruption and acting as a deterrent. It also has the force of the law under the Public Interest Disclosure Act 1998. The Act protects those who disclose facts to protect 'the public interest' and came into force in January 1999. In a procurement context the Act could be reasonably expected to cover the following disclosure of malpractice:

- **Bid rigging**: any type of collusive action between contractors during a bidding process. It includes the submission of false bids to artificially raise prices, the creation of fake companies, and taking turns to submit 'low bids' after bidders exchange information.
- **Bribery**: the offering, giving, receiving, or soliciting of any thing of value either in the UK or overseas to influence an action of an official.
- **Collusion**: two or more parties acting together to defraud a person or an organization.
- **Corruption**: the offering, giving, receiving, or soliciting of anything of value to influence the action of a public official whether in the UK or overseas.
- **Theft**: the fraudulent taking of property belonging to another, with intent to permanently deprive the owner of the property.

The act of whistle-blowing must satisfy a number of criteria for reasonableness. For example, reasonableness includes situations where the whistle-blower should have raised his concern with the employer or prescribed regulator but reasonably believed he would be victimized by so doing. It might also apply where the whistle-blower reasonably believed there would be a cover-up. If these conditions are met and a tribunal is satisfied that the disclosure was reasonable, the whistle-blower will be protected.

Malicious tale-telling, true or false, or breaking company confidentiality in an unwarranted fashion with ulterior motives is unlikely to be considered reasonable, and the whistle-blower will not be protected. Normal recompense in terms of actions for libel, slander, damages and dismissal could then apply against the whistle-blower.

If organizations do wish to use whistle-blowing as a means of protecting themselves against corruption and fraud they need to introduce measures to convince staff of their sincerity:

- Involve staff, establish a common culture of right and wrong. Explain the effects that fraud and corruption could have on the organization, its effects on their jobs and the service they provide.
- When serious malpractice is found (whether by employees or suppliers), deal with it seriously and promptly. Remember it cannot be expected that staff practise higher standards than those the organization applies.
- Make clear that the organization is committed to tackling fraud and abuse, whether the perpetrators are inside or outside. In this context it applauds and supports whistle-blowers.
- Staff should clearly know what practices are unacceptable. Treat the ethical code very seriously.
- Make it clear that the malicious use of whistle-blowing cannot be tolerated as there are legal implications for both parties. Publish a code to clarify the boundaries of acceptability.

Without adopting these basic measures it would be unrealistic to expect most employees to take the risk of raising their heads above the parapet and possibly incuring the wrath of both their colleagues and management.

ETHICAL LEADERSHIP

It would appear logical for the profession to show leadership by taking the moral high ground with regard to business ethics and using it as a marketing USP or UPB, because purchasing can largely choose whom it does business with. However, a more pragmatic approach to stick to the supply side may need to be adopted in some organizations where, because of intense international competition, the sales side cannot afford to adopt such a seemingly pious approach.

Chapter summary

- Currently there are no practical methods of measuring an individual's tendency to defraud.

- Most inducements offered to buyers amount to bribery.

- Ethical codes can help protect both the organization and the individual.

- Effective controls, particularly concerning segregation of duties and supplier accreditation, are essential.

- Constant vigilance should be second nature – one 'bad apple' can spoil in an instant years of hard work in building a reputation for impeccable business ethics.

- The organization's attitude to whistle-blowing requires careful management.

CHAPTER 14

CONCLUSIONS

DIRECTION

There are three golden rules to delivering a memorable presentation – firstly tell 'em what you are going to tell 'em, secondly tell 'em and thirdly tell 'em again what you have just told 'em! Working along similar lines this concluding chapter must inevitably follow the third golden rule – tell 'em what you have just told 'em. However, as this book has laboured to emphasize the strategic importance of the Purchasing function, it may also be as well to attempt to crystal ball gaze the future of our profession. On this matter it was a very wise person indeed who said that the only certain predication that could be made about future change is that there would be change, and if this sounds as if I may be hedging my bets, so be it. If one looks back, our experience tends to confirm this picture of the unpredictable nature of change. In my case I originally trained in the printing industry taking a shop floor apprenticeship. My company offered every encouragement to gain qualifications at the London College of Printing and as I reached the end of my apprenticeship high wages beckoned because at the time the printers, miners and steelworkers were the best paid in the country. However, I began to realize that this job was not for me because radical change was on the horizon. It was fairly obvious at the time that the stranglehold that the trade unions exerted on management, politicians and the country at large could not be allowed to continue. No one predicted that in the printing industry this would come about by Eddie Shah and Rupert Murdoch relocating the whole of Fleet Street and changing the printing processes that had been used for 150 years. At the same time some technical change was being introduced in my neck of the woods with the use of electronics for colour separations. However, I still marvel that a colour correction job that would the have taken a skilled craftsman a week to perform in my time can now be undertaken in just a few minutes by anyone who is computer literate and has a basic knowledge of photography. Plus the quality is far superior.

TELL 'EM AGAIN

Coming back to the 'tell 'em again' theme: in general the profession continues to make progress in gaining more power and influence, as ever-increasing competition forces top management to consider the added contribution that we can make to increase both competitive advantage and bottom line contribution. However, progress in this context encapsulates a very wide range, is very patchy and varies tremendously across different organizations. Some are still in the Stone Age where buyers are in truth mere administrative order placers to the other extreme of high-tech organizations where Purchasing is recognised as an essential strategic team member vital to business success. Most buyers are, however, employed by organizations that fall into the middle ground of business recognition and for them it is important that their function raises its profile. The very point of this book is to help achieve this ambition.

The first step on the road is to step back and take a cool calculated look at the current positioning of the Purchasing function and then form a judgement of what can be realistically achieved within that particular organization in the short, medium and long term. It is important to be brutally realistic because if, say, the organization is run by 'robber baron' type directors who thrive on permanent internal conflict, then perhaps it is better to either keep your head down or alternatively cut and run. In other words, the art of the possible is a very important consideration when formulating positioning planning.

In truth, as mentioned earlier in the book, the aspiration to raise profile is nothing new but as we have not succeeded that well in the past it is now time to adopt new methods to achieve our goals. When we think that Purchasing is really operating as a business within a business it rapidly becomes apparent that like any other modern business it is impossible to succeed without having an effective sales and marketing operation in place.

The crux of marketing is to identify the real wants and needs of customers and then design ways of satisfying these desires. Operating Purchasing as a business brings the realization that we have internal customers and should we not supply a service that *they* (not us) think is first class, then how can we ever begin to obtain the respect of business colleagues? The initial 'turning over of the stones' when a customer survey is undertaken will inevitably reveal some unpleasant and unexpected surprises that may prove to be very uncomfortable. Phrases such as 'Purchasing – a waste of space', 'Purchasing – just a bottleneck' or 'Purchasing – time wasting bureaucrats' are not uncommon. Yes, much of this customer opinion will consist of unfair and subjective feelings but they must nevertheless be addressed pragmatically and creatively as a key part of any marketing plan. A classic example of what can be achieved is how Volkswagen in a relatively short time has changed public perception of the Skoda brand.

Just because they are meeting sales people all the time many buyers quite erroneously think that they know all about selling. Alas, if this were only half-true, the purchasing function would have long ago elevated itself to a position of far greater importance. All buyers should therefore go on sales training courses because then they would begin to realize how little they really know about how they are often being manipulated during the buying/ selling process. The art of selling consists largely of being good at dealing with people. It is about building relationships, finding out what makes people tick, manipulation and even the massaging of egos. Not many of us find it easy to do these things, especially if the contact is not friendly. Small wonder therefore that buyers focus on dealing with apparently admiring suppliers, rather than selling internally to difficult and demanding customers. Let us therefore spend more time looking inwards rather than outwards. After all, it is not suppliers who pay our wages.

Spending insufficient time on our customers has led them to having little appreciation of the benefits that we can bring them. We have effectively been hiding our light under a bushel for far too long because we fail to project our achievements in a manner that the organization can readily appreciate. Employing new ways to measure activity and report on it in a more meaningful business language, such as via a profit and loss account of the purchasing business can be used to boost credibility. This is not to denigrate the many tried and tested techniques that we already employ to measure and improve performance, it is just that we need to find more sexy ways of promoting them to our customer colleagues. After all, how many of them find our cost saving figures exciting or even believable? The usual comment is 'OK but why then have we been paying over the odds before?' Gently educating and involving them to appreciate the beneficial role that Purchasing can play in their world is necessary. Let us therefore take a lead in co-operation projects such as more use of cross-functional teams, supplier conferences and short-term inter-departmental job swaps.

Purchasing does have an array of skills that are useful to the organization. For instance, we are well placed to become the acknowledged experts and the moral and ethical guardians of honest business practices. What is now required is the adoption of new tricks to sell these skills to ensure their take-up. To some a requirement for knowledge of body language is a physiological step too far. However, in a profession that inevitably leans heavily on human interaction this knowledge can help in our everyday buying work as well helping us to master the art of selling.

The changes required to produce an invite to the top table involve:

- considering current and potential positioning;
- thinking and acting strategically;
- researching customer real and perceived desires;
- producing and implementing a marketing and sales plan;
- training in new skills such as selling techniques and the understanding of body language;
- increasing market share;
- maintaining a culture of continuous improvement;
- delivering more meaningful management information.

THE IMPACT OF GLOBALIZATION

The world never stands still, so once these goals have been achieved, where are we moving to? What of the future? One obvious factor is the globalization of supply chains and the outsourcing of low level activity to far-flung regions of the planet. Not many of us would actually prefer to talk to a call centre in India, so when this outsourcing appears to be purely for cost reasons never mind the customer quality expectations, the question must be raised, will there be a backlash? Perhaps some of these projects are not turning out to be as successful as was first envisaged because often in the service business arena Purchasing is still only involved at the margins. With regard to buying manufactured goods from the developing world, this trend seems to be flying in the face of the previously perceived wisdom of the merits of lean manufacturing – small-batch personalized manufacture to supply instant demand with no stockholding. Buying from the Far East involves much longer lead times than local manufacture. Admittedly the cost of manufacture is much lower but logistical costs will continue to rise as the price of oil is set to constantly increase as Third World demand takes off. Add to this the effects on extended fragile supply chains of political crises, global climate change and energy shortages and it does appear that organizations that rely on Third World manufacturing capacity are carrying a considerable risk burden. For instance, it is not inconceivable that a country like China, that has a veneer of capitalism underlain with heavy state control, could at some time in the future collapse into chaos and revolution as pressures between bureaucratic state and private enterprise become intolerable.

The stampede to low-cost sourcing on the other side of the world is unstoppable at the moment because the cost-saving opportunities are so irresistible. However, I would counsel that organizations that put all their eggs in one basket are placing the future of their business at too high a risk. Inevitably a global problem will arise which will result in companies that have had the foresight to spread their supply base both internationally and locally will then have a massive competitive advantage. There may even be a case for mothballing some elements of local production rather than lose them forever by throwing them on the scrapheap. However, whatever the international problem, there is a major new role for purchasing management to play in leading contingency planning teams to consider and instigate ways to counteract the myriad risks that globalization of the supply chain bring.

Looking further ahead, what will the world look like to our grandchildren? Mass communication brings an awareness and hunger for the delights of consumerism to every single person on the planet and once the genie starts coming out of the bottle it can never be put back. A decade ago in China the universal mode of transport was the bicycle, now already it is becoming the car. How long before this becomes the norm for all mankind? Will this lead to a levelling-up of the general standard of living or will the West be forced to lower its consumer expectations? The rising global birth and survival rate, universal consumerism, depletion of natural resources and inevitable climate change appear to be wholly incompatible. All that can be said is that this combination of circumstances must lead to major change but what this change will actually be is impossible for anyone to predict.

At this point, readers may be wondering why a book about purchasing should be pursuing such a philosophical debate? Well, as buyers our role tends to be to grease the wheels of consumerism, so occasionally perhaps there is no harm in considering the effects that our endeavours may be having on the future. My first job in buying was for a greetings card company. I remember that occasionally I asked myself what was I doing working for a company that produced such a mundane and basically unnecessary product? It would have been far better working in a business that actually benefited mankind, but if truth be known I had a young family to keep and the job was teaching me a great deal about the art of buying.

It would be interesting to know how many of us currently working in the profession feels the same way that I did so many years ago. I guess it all goes to show that at times in our career, work sometimes consists of just getting on with it, though one must always be alive and alert to seeking and taking opportunities that arise. In partial mitigation I only stayed in the job for a year before moving on.

TRAINING AND DEVELOPMENT

As the pace of change continues to constantly accelerate, the need for personal development becomes ever more important if individuals have any chance of keeping pace. There is a question, however, whether the professional bodies that traditionally lead the way can broaden their horizons sufficiently to take into account the speed of change. With the exception of CIPS co-operation with its Australian counterpart and a membership drive in Africa and the Far East, professional bodies seem to have largely ignored the commercial trend for globalization. For instance, there are now no barriers to any EC citizen of one country working in any other EC member country. However, there are no recognised cross-border purchasing qualifications and professional standards. This must inhibit opportunity and the free movement of labour. There is therefore a need for more cross-border co-operation and amalgamation of professional bodies to produce common standards. It is unlikely to happen, however, unless members push their paid and elected officials very hard because of the vested interests that stand in the way such as self-interest, jingoism, politics, job protection and egos.

TECHNOLOGY

The profession is fortunate because much of the administration that formerly bogged down buyers can now be taken care of by the computerization of repetitive processes. For many years there have been excellent software packages on the market that if fully integrated with accounts payable can efficiently automate the whole requisition to pay process. It is amazing therefore that many purchasing departments are still not using them to their full potential. For instance, in September 2005 the *Daily Telegraph* published an article that highlighted research by Exor Management Services showing inefficiency in invoice payment by local authorities. Instead of aggregating invoices for monthly payment many are paying them individually. When payments were tracked across fifty local authorities over a twelve-month period it was found that the top ten suppliers had received a massive 243 864 individual payments. Top of the list was British Telecom who had received 41 894 individual payments. What a pain for them and what a waste of money when the use of technology would make it simple to aggregate by month and thus reduce the number of payments to a mere 600. Assuming that it costs on average £50 to process and pay an invoice, annual savings on the BT account alone would amount to over £2 million. What are the buyers and finance staff playing at? Is it a case oh 'ah well' it is only the council taxpayers' money?

I must confess to being a fan of eCommerce in general and reverse auctions in particular but not necessarily as be-all and end-all solutions but as other valuable tools to be added to the professional buyers' armoury. In 2004 the Strategic Procurement Review 2004 published by Market Focus Research revealed that only 13 per cent of respondents had a fully implemented eCommerce strategy. Admittedly the figures are slightly out of date but there must still be a long way to go before the use of eCommerce and its future derivatives become universal.

A technological purchasing wish that is not being fulfilled at the moment is a Google-type search engine especially designed for professional buyers that would list every medium to large source of supply in the world. To date, many attempts have been made without any of them taking off because they have not had the strength in depth required. Nevertheless it is an easy prediction to make that sooner or later someone will come up with the perfect solution.

THE FUTURE FOR PURCHASING PROFESSIONALS

In the short- to medium-term, career prospects appear good as more and more top management appreciate the benefits that purchasing professionals bring to their business. Increasing salary levels, particularly for well qualified people with state of the art experience, is an obvious example of the progress being made. To continue the trend, however, does depend on increasing people skills outside the narrow procurement remit to include areas such as general management, finance, sales and marketing. A progressive outlook and a willingness to undertake continuous self-improvement programmes will be absolutely essential to keep abreast of the ever-increasing pace of change.

Senior purchasing managers that have managed to establish their position at the top tables are already finding that they need to sharpen their total all-round business knowledge. It is no longer sufficient for them to sit at top-level meetings and just contribute their pearls of procurement wisdom because corporate decision making means that they need to understand and contribute to all aspects of business strategy. This is also happening at lower levels in organizations where cross-functional team working has already become an established fact of life.

It is doubtful whether the traditional departmental way of running businesses can survive the onslaught of all this continuous change. We all know and experience that departmental boxes such as purchasing, finance, human resources, sales, marketing and so on can be extremely divisive and liable to constant political manoeuvring. Big organizations are particularly susceptible to being run by departmental 'Robber Barons' who appear to be more interested in territorial protection rather than the good of the organization. These artificial boundaries can also act as career straightjackets, particularly for intelligent well qualified graduates. Intense international competition is driving root-and-branch consideration of the way that we organize business and it is obvious that the little boxes set-up do not stack up too well in the efficiency stakes. Indeed it is a little surprising that these divisions have survived untouched for so long.

Organizations have already begun to wonder if they really need the hassle of managing service departments in-house. Departments such as human resources, financial administration and even dare I say it – routine purchasing – can easily be outsourced. This has already happened in some hotel chains where everything has been outsourced except taking the bookings and the money from the customer. Most internal service areas experience peaks and troughs in their workload so are quite often overstaffed at quieter periods. Under these circumstances outsourcing to specialists can therefore be more efficient. Even if routine purchasing is considered to be core to the business the adoption of eCommerce is leading to the automating, streamlining and simplifying much of the work, leading to a reduction of the skill levels required.

In the longer term, therefore, the way we currently organize business cannot possibly be sustained. The breakdown in the slow response departmental structure will do away with most of the specialist jobs that are currently jealously guarded and along with it will go a whole sector of qualifications, professional institutes and specialist training. It is envisaged that in future as global competition and time to market pressures intensify business will be run along project management lines, not departmental boxes. Management teams will run business on a project by project basis, each individually run and costed. One project will stand and fall on, say, marketing success whereas the next may depend on negotiating the right supply deal in the Far East. The skill set required to work in this new project environment will be very different, as a much broader knowledge of the whole business will be essential.

If twenty-something ambitious youngsters currently studying for their CIPS qualifications think that their career path will lay in a steady progression from buyer, to senior buyer, to purchasing manger, to purchasing director – think again. Sure, currently it is good to aim for full membership of CIPS because it does provide a theoretical introduction to other areas of business. After that an MBA is already becoming essential. My advice would be to gain experience beyond purchasing as soon as possible, for instance, by pushing hard for secondments to other departments. Graduates should also seek the graduate training schemes that offer the widest possible in-depth business experience.

To some that are a bit older and wondering how they will fit into the new work management system, I say do not despair too soon. Yes, change is speeding up, but quite often nothing ever happens quite as quickly as we anticipate. Consider for instance, even the thrusting *enfant terrible* of technology – the mobile phone – has taken around twenty years to conquer the globe and it will take NASA at least thirty-six years to repeat the first manned moon landing.

The progress of purchasing development on the ground is so varied across market sectors and organizations that on average, it will probably be at the lower end of the speed of change continuum. Finally, to return to the main thrust of the book, it is therefore very reassuring to envisage that the progressive practices advocated will be valid and applicable to most organizations for the next twenty years.

A SAMPLE SET OF SUPPLIER EVALUATION AND ACCREDITATION PROCEDURES

This sample cuts out all the hard work normally involved in creating a new set of procedures because it can easily be adapted to suit your organization. Also, very importantly, using a set of standard procedures like this will demonstrate purchasing professionalism to the marketplace and prove to existing and potential suppliers that they are being treated fairly and objectively. In addition it forms the basis for the introduction of a continuous improvement Kaizen-type programme.

- Telephone sales call received – verbally invite potential suppliers to send information on their company as listed in letter 1.
- Introductory letter received – send standard letter 1 requesting additional information.
- Match response to Accreditation requirements.
- Response does not meet requirements – send standard letter 2.
- Response does meet requirements – send standard letter 3 to arrange supplier visit.
- Site visit – complete form 1, the Supplier Visit Record.
- If requirements listed in form 1 are not satisfactory, send standard decline letter 4 giving rationale.
- Requirements are met – send potential supplier form 2, the Vendor Appraisal form.
- After completed form is returned apply rating compared to selection standards using form 3, the Supplier Accreditation form.
- Requirements not met – send decline letter 6 with rationale.
- Requirements met but sufficient similarly qualified suppliers in portfolio – send standard letter 7.
- Requirements met and potentially a better supplier than existing portfolio – send standard letter 8. Arrange for senior management visit if appropriate

- Senior management decision to decline – send standard decline letter 9 giving rationale.
- Senior management decision to accept – send standard letter 10 and complete form 4, Supplier Accreditation form.
- Set up supplier on approved supplier list in portfolio.

STANDARD LETTER 1
(A polite reply to an initial sales contact)

> Subject – Supplier Evaluation
>
> Dear xxxx
> Thank you for making contact with Group Purchasing.
>
> We would request that you supply further details regarding the nature of your company's business, for example, Latest Report & Accounts, Corporate Brochure, Product file and full plant list (if appropriate).
>
> This information will assist us in assessing how closely your company's facility matches our requirements.
>
> Yours sincerely,

STANDARD LETTER 2
(A polite decline)

> Subject – Supplier Evaluation
>
> Dear xxxx
> Thank you for supplying information regarding your company.
>
> We regret to inform you that your company has not been selected as a supplier as we currently have sufficient good suppliers in your field. However your company details will be held on file and should our needs change we will contact you.
>
> May we ask that you keep us appraised of any significant changes within your company and the services it is able to offer. We would also like to take this opportunity to wish you every success in the future.
>
> Yours sincerely,

A similar letter could be used to decline if they are agents or middlemen and it is your policy to only deal direct with manufacturers. Similarly if they cannot provide a nationwide service or are not suitably ISO accredited and so on. The main point is to supply them with a valid reason for turning them down. Do not give them the impression that it is merely on a buyer's whim.

STANDARD LETTER 3
(Arrange supplier visit)

Subject – Supplier Evaluation leading to possible Accreditation

Dear xxxx
Further to our recent correspondence, we would like to arrange a visit to view your premises and have further discussions on our requirements.

Please contact the undersigned to arrange a mutually convenient time and date.

Yours sincerely,

STANDARD LETTER 4 – WITH RATIONALE
(Decline after visit)

Subject – Supplier Evaluation

Dear xxxx
Thank you for the courtesy shown on my recent visit.

We regret to inform you that your company has not been selected as an approved supplier at this time for the following reasons:

-
-
-

However should the situation change, please contact us and we will review our decision.

We would also like to take this opportunity to wish you every success in the future.

Yours sincerely,

STANDARD FORM 1
(Supplier visit record)

Supplier visit record

Company name and address	Other premises and companies in the same group

Telephone numbers, emails, websites

Contacts:

Managing Director:	Sales Director:
Production Manager:	Financial Director:
Account Manager:	Day-to-day contact:
Other relevant personnel	

Purpose of visit

Commodities supplied

Equipment and premises condition

Workflow and housekeeping

Commodities supplied

Quality assurance

Financial health

Attitude and culture

Visit completed by	Visit completed by

STANDARD LETTER 5
(Site visit requirements are met) to accompany Form 2

Subject – Supplier Evaluation and Accreditation

Dear xxxx
Thank you for the courtesy shown on my recent visit.

We think that you may be a suitable supplier to be added to our approved supplier list. However, to help us complete our assessment please complete all the sections of the enclosed Supplier Evaluation form and return it to the undersigned.

All information supplied will be treated in the strictest confidence and used only in conjunction with our Supplier Accreditation process.

Yours sincerely,

STANDARD LETTER 6
(Decline letter with rationale)

Subject: Supplier Accreditation

Dear xxxx
Many thanks for the courtesy shown on my recent visit and for completing our Supplier Evaluation form.

In this instance we regret that your company has not been selected as an approved supplier as you have not reached our standards in the following areas:

-
-

Should this situation change in the future please contact us to review our decision.

Yours sincerely,

STANDARD FORM 2
(Supplier evaluation)

Supplier evaluation

SECTION A. Company Data

Name of business	Are you a manufacturer?

Nature of business

Business address	Telephone No Email Website

Limited company registration number

How long has the company been established?

Name and address of parent company (if applicable)

Please supply organizational charts, by department, for your Company and also by company if part of a group

Please supply addresses of other sales offices in the group that we should be aware of including staff names and contact details

SECTION B. Financial Data

Annual turnover	Your company	Parent company
Net profit	Your company	Parent company

Please also forward a copy of your last reports and accounts

Are your premises leasehold, rented or freehold?

If leasehold, number of years remaining

If freehold, age of property

STANDARD FORM 2
(Supplier evaluation, continued)

Supplier evaluation

SECTION C. Personnel

Number of employees

Employee breakdown

Sales ☐   Production and design ☐   Admin. and accounts ☐

Others please specify

Personnel contacts

SALES	Name: Position:
PRODUCTION	Name: Position:
FINANCE	Name: Position:

Managing Director:

Sales Director:

Production Director:

Please also supply an organization chart, showing the company structure for key personnel

SECTION D. Transport and delivery

Own transport or contracted?

Number of warehouses and locations

Do you usually charge extra for delivery?

STANDARD FORM 2
(Supplier evaluation, continued)

Supplier evaluation

SECTION E. Administration

Documentation:
Please supply samples of: (1) an invoice
                       (2) an order acknowledgment
                       (3) standard terms and conditions
                       (4) delivery note

Can you also handle all this administration electronically and also specify which eCommerce software you employ?

Please state address for
receipt of purchase orders

Please state address for
invoice payment

If you accept payment by BACS, please provide the following instruction

Name of bank   Sort code

Bank account number

SECTION F. Quality assurance

Please supply a brief description of the internal quality assurance procedures you operate.

Also, provide details of your ISO Certifications plus any other recognized standards you are accredited to.

Supply details of your environmental policies. *Note: it may be applicable to ask for ethical policies if your company operates a strict ethical code.*

Please send an up-to-date plant list, stating the age of equipment.

STANDARD FORM 2
(Supplier evaluation, concluded)

Supplier evaluation

REFERENCES

Please state some of your major customers, their line of business and their percentage of your company turnover. *Note: we promise not to contact any of these customers without first contacting you to obtain your express permission.*

(1) Company name and address, contact telephone number, line of business and percentage company turnover

(2) Company name and address, contact telephone number, line of business and percentage company turnover

(3) Company name and address, contact telephone number, line of business and percentage company turnover

(4) Company name and address, contact telephone number, line of business and percentage company turnover

Note for buyers – Depending on your purchasing power at this stage of the accreditation process, suppliers may be reluctant to supply details of the major customer's spending, therefore, you may be forced to seek references later when you can dangle the prospect of them definitely obtaining some of your business.

STANDARD LETTER 7
(Decline letter to a promising company)

Subject: Supplier Accreditation

Dear xxxx
Many thanks for the courtesy shown on my recent visit and for completing our Supplier Evaluation form.

We regret to inform you that unfortunately your Company has not been added to our approved supplier list at this time despite you fulfilling most of the criteria we seek. This is because we have sufficient satisfactory suppliers of the services you offer at present. However you are in a prominent position on our reserve list and should the situation change we will certainly contact you.

Thanks again for your co-operation and we will be retaining full details of your organisation on our files pending future requirements.

Yours sincerely,

STANDARD LETTER 8
(Senior Management visit letter to a promising company)

Subject: Supplier Accreditation

Dear xxxx
Many thanks for the courtesy shown on my recent visit and for completing our Supplier Evaluation form.

Your response is interesting and we would now like to arrange for our Senior Manager .... (name) who is responsible for this procurement area to visit you at a mutually convenient time.

Please telephone...................... or email...................... to arrange this.

Yours sincerely,

STANDARD FORM 3
(Supplier evaluation, continued)

Supplier accreditation

Company name and address

Product groups and systems vendor number

Rating

Financial:

Quality:

Equipment, technology, premises, culture:

Evaluation by:

Signed: ....

Senior Manager .... (Date)

Note: The evaluation, especially the rating, needs to be discussed and agreed by the Buyer and Senior Manager involved.

STANDARD LETTER 9
(Senior Management decline letter)

Subject: Supplier Accreditation

Dear xxxx
Many thanks for the courtesy you showed me on my recent very interesting visit. Unfortunately despite having many of the qualities we are seeking you have not been selected as Group Purchasing Supplier at this time for the following reasons:

-
-

Should the situation change please contact me and we will be pleased to review our decision.

I should also like to take this opportunity to wish you every success in the future and trust that we will meet again.

Yours sincerely,

STANDARD LETTER 10
(Senior Management Accreditation confirmation letter)

Subject: Supplier Accreditation

Dear xxxx
I trust that I am the bearer of good news. Further to recent visits by myself and .... I am pleased to tell you that your Company has passed all our accreditation hurdles with flying colours and you have been selected to be a Group Purchasing approved supplier.

Your Accreditation will be reviewed on an annual basis using information obtained from our supplier rating system. Our buyers will provide you with details of this scheme as we place orders or contracts with you.

Meanwhile it only remains for me to welcome you as a new supplier with the wish that the relationship turns out to be most beneficial for both our respective organisations.

Yours sincerely,

It now only remains for the new supplier to be set up on the internal computer systems. It is essential to maintain formal records of this to reduce the possibility of fraud by the setting-up of unauthorised suppliers by dishonest buyers.

STANDARD FORM 4
Approved supplier set-up authorization

Approved supplier set-up authorization accreditation
Company name and address
Payment address (if different)
Contact details, phone numbers, names, emails, etc.

Our normal payment terms

Settlement discount details

Approved commodities to be supplied with computer coding categories

AUTHORIZED BY:

Buyer .... Signed: .... (Date) ....

Senior Buyer .... Signed: .... (Date) ....

Senior Manager .... Signed: .... (Date) ....
(after checking entry on computer)

COMPUTER INPUT BY:
Buyer .... Signed: .... (Date) ....

SUPPLIER NUMBER

A SAMPLE SET OF SUPPLIER RATING PROCEDURES

These can of course be adapted to suit any particular organizational circumstance.

SEQUENCE OF EVENTS FOR STRATEGICALLY IMPORTANT WORK TO BE SUPPLIER RATED

1. Monitoring form one completed for each order/contract placed. The completion of this form is the responsibility of the buyer concerned who must ensure that the information completed is factual, concise and unbiased. The work is not scored at this stage, form one is used to record facts as they occur.

2. Monthly team meeting of buyers involved in each commodity grouping to review the collection of form 1s to ensure unanimity and agreement regarding the actual performance of each supplier that is rated. It is also used to make sure that they are all singing from the same hymn sheet when they agree a score for each completed order/contract by completing form 2 – Supplier Scoring form. The meeting is usually chaired by the senior buyer who also signs off the form to signal team consensus.

3. The senior buyer for each section produces the monthly rating (using standard form 3 – Consolidated Supplier monthly rating form) for each supplier based on averaging the scores. (Total scores listed on all relevant forms divided by the number of orders/contracts rated). If severe problems are indicated the senior buyer may decide to call in the supplier at this early stage to discuss immediate corrective action. Hopefully this is not normally required.

4. Quarterly letters (see standard letters 1 or 2) are despatched to suppliers showing their quarterly rating, broken down by month.

The letters differ slightly depending whether their ratings are satisfactory or not.

5. Quarterly review meeting held with all suppliers. The personnel to attend should remain flexible. For instance, a review meeting to suppliers who have received letter one may require the big guns to be wheeled out to indicate the seriousness that problems are taken and to ensure swift corrective action is undertaken. Suppliers that have received letter 2 may only require a couple of buyers to attend the meeting to discuss continuous improvements with their peers from the supplier.

6. Further more frequent meetings may need to take place with problem suppliers to monitor progress of corrective action plans.

7. After twelve months all buyers and purchasing management are involved in reviewing results and selecting and presenting Supplier of the Year awards.

STANDARD FORM 1

(Supplier monitoring form for rating purposes)

Supplier monitoring form for rating purposes

Commodity buying team

Buyer responsible

Supplier and supplier number

Product or service purchased

Order/contact number and date

Delivery satisfaction

Quality

Complaints

Flexibility

Communication

Administration

Pricing

Note: This form is completed factually by the buyer as the order/contract is progressed by the supplier

STANDARD FORM 2
(Supplier scoring form by individual order)

Supplier scoring form by individual order

Commodity buying team

Buyer responsible

Supplier and supplier number

Product or service purchased

Order/contact number and date

CRITERIA			Max score	Actual score
DELIVERY		Score		
	On time	☐	☐	☐
	Presentation	☐		
	Documentation	☐		
QUALITY		Score		
	Product	☐	☐	☐
	Service quality	☐		
COMPLAINTS		Score		
	Customer	☐	☐	☐
	Complaint handling	☐		
FLEXIBILITY		Score		
	Responsiveness	☐	☐	☐
	Change management	☐		
COMMUNICATION		Score		
	Progress reporting	☐	☐	☐
	Rep. availability	☐		
	Oral and written	☐		
ADMINISTRATION		Score		
	Accuracy	☐	☐	☐
	Rep. availability	☐		
PRICING		Score		
	Competitive	☐	☐	☐
	Estimate turnaround	☐		
	Flexible	☐		

TOTALS

Buyer (signature and date) .... (Date) ....
Senior Buyer (signature and date) .... (Date) ....

STANDARD FORM 3
(Consolidated supplier monthly rating form)

Consolidated supplier monthly rating form

Commodity grouping   Supplier name and number

QUALITY   Max score   [50]

0 – 39 = D
40 – 45 = C
46 – 48 = B
49 – 50 = A   Actual score   [   ]

SERVICE   Max score   [40]

0 – 29 = D
30 – 35 = C
36 – 38 = B
39 – 40 = A   Actual score   [   ]

PRICE   Max score   [10]

0 – 4   = D
5 – 6   = C
7 – 8   = B
9 – 10 = A   Actual score   [   ]

PRICE   [   ]   QUALITY   [   ]   SERVICE   [   ]

RATING FOR THE MONTH OF ....

Senior Buyer (signature and date)   ....   (Date) ....
Senior Manager (signature and date) ....   (Date) ....

Note: the figures are merely nominal. They will change according to the initial commodity assessment

STANDARD LETTER 1
(Warning that rating is not satisfactory)

Subject – Supplier Rating

Dear xxxx
This letter is to deliver your quarterly supplier rating results. They are as follows:

MONTH	PRICE	QUALITY	SERVICE
January	B	D	C
February	B	C	B
March	B	D	B

You will no doubt be as concerned as we are about the quality that has been delivered during the past quarter. Let us therefore meet as soon as possible to produce a joint action plan to address our quality concerns.

Yours sincerely,

STANDARD LETTER 2
(Satisfactory supplier rating results)

Subject – Supplier Rating

Dear xxxx
This letter is to deliver your quarterly supplier rating results. They are as follows:

MONTH	PRICE	QUALITY	SERVICE
January	B	A	C
February	B	B	B
March	B	A	A

Like us you we trust that you will be pleased with you quarterly rating results. Let us now look forward to discussing them at our quarterly continuous improvement meeting.

Yours sincerely,

INDEX